EASY
ENTERTAINING
AT HOME

Mapletini: Mix 1½ ounces Bulleit® bourbon, 1 teaspoon maple syrup, and 1 dash vanilla extract in a shaker with cracked ice. Strain into a tumbler filled midway with cracked ice. Top with 3 ounces soda water. Garnish with maple candy. Makes 1 drink.

Sandra Lee

EASY
ENTERTAINING
AT HOME

This book belongs to:

 SL BOOKS
sandralee.com

 HYPERION
NEW YORK

Lee, Sandra.
 Easy entertaining at home : cocktails, finger foods, and creative ideas for year-round celebrations / Sandra Lee. — 1st ed.
  p. cm.
  ISBN 978-1-4013-1080-6 (pbk.)
1. Entertaining. 2. Beverages. 3. Cookbooks. I. Title.
 TX731.L44 2011
 642.4092—dc23
  2011023565

Hyperion books are available for special promotions and premiums. For details contact the HarperCollins Special Markets Department in the New York office at 212-207-7528, fax 212-207-7222, or email spsales@harpercollins.com.

FIRST EDITION

10 9 8 7 6 5 4 3 2 1

SUSTAINABLE FORESTRY INITIATIVE
Certified Fiber Sourcing
www.sfiprogram.org

THIS LABEL APPLIES TO TEXT STOCK

We try to produce the most beautiful books possible, and we are also extremely concerned about the impact of our manufacturing process on the forests of the world and the environment as a whole. Accordingly, we've made sure that all of the paper we use has been certified as coming from forests that are managed, to ensure the protection of the people and wildlife dependent upon them.

White Gown Add 1¼ ounces Captain Morgan® Parrot Bay Coconut Rum, 1 ounce milk, and 5 ounces pineapple juice to a blender. Blend 10–15 seconds and pour into a tall glass filled with crushed iced. Garnish with a mint sprig. Makes 1 drink.

Vintage Chic Margarita (as seen on cover) Add 1½ ounces Jose Cuervo® Especial Gold tequila, 3 ounces Jose Cuervo® Lime Margarita Mix, 1 handful fresh strawberries, and 4 ounces crushed ice to a blender, and blend until smooth. Pour into glass. Makes 1 drink.

Dedication

To all of the wonderful hosts and entertainers who make every get-together with family and friends a celebration to remember. Thank you and cheers to those who participate in "Cocktailing for a Cause" and for joining me in making a difference. Please let these new recipes and helpful tips inspire you to host more fund-raising parties.

Golden Accessory Fill a pitcher halfway with ice. Add 6 ounces Jose Cuervo® Especial Gold tequila, 8 ounces Jose Cuervo® Lime Margarita Mix, 8 ounces orange juice, and 4 teaspoons sugar. Stir well. Mix with slices of 1 orange. Makes 4 drinks.

Glitterati Margarita Fill a pitcher halfway with ice. Add 6 ounces Jose Cuervo® Especial Gold tequila, 8 ounces Jose Cuervo® Strawberry Lime Margarita Mix, 8 ounces pineapple juice, and 4 teaspoons sugar. Stir well. Mix with slices of 1 lemon. Makes 4 drinks.

Contents

JUNE

JULY

AUGUST

From Sandra

Welcome to the world of *Easy Entertaining,* where gatherings and get-togethers are a stress-free pleasure. When I entertain, I like to include my friends, family, and even the family pets. I am not the type of person to place the family dog behind the closed door of a bedroom, or lock my beautiful cockatoo, Phoenix, in a cage. Part of making people feel at home is having your home be as it is, welcoming and festive, so I include everyone.

When I first started throwing parties, I took on entertaining with great excitement and passion. I was going to be the best host my friends had ever seen. Talk about stressing yourself out! I learned how to throw a great bash two ways, the hard way and the easy way. I can assure you that the easy way is much more enjoyable. The most important lesson I learned was that guests come to see the host. The food and drinks are important, but not as important as the mood your guests are greeted with, the fun and festive atmosphere you provide, and the energy of the room.

I rarely throw big sit-down dinners or luncheons, unless it's a holiday. I tend to host small gatherings for ten people or less, and I always think "do-able"—easy al fresco, or an upscale pasta, pizza, and salad party. But what's always in favor is a cocktail-and-appetizer soiree, and that is why this book is filled with so many incredible combinations, such as Minty Mojito and Capri Bites; Blushing Sangria and Roasted Pepper Steak Skews; and Porch Swing Ice Tea and Shoreline Salmon Sliders.

The most important thing to remember is to not take on too much, and to always be organized so you're not overwhelmed and stressed at the last minute. Gatherings and get-togethers have never been easier than with this new at-home entertaining book.

Parties should be a pleasure for all, including the host. And with this book, everyone can entertain with ease.

Cheers to a sweet soirée!

Couture Colada Add ¾ ounce Godiva®
Chocolate liqueur, ¼ ounce Cîroc®
vodka, and 1 cup milk in ice-filled rocks
glass and stir. Makes 1 drink.

Setting the bar with premium spirits

Prepared cocktails—just pour over ice

Raspberry Lemonade Mash ½ cup
raspberries and ¾ cup sugar together
and let sit at room temperature to
thaw and bring out their juices. Set a
sieve over a pitcher and juice 4 lemons.
Rinse sieve. Push raspberry mixture
through sieve with a rubber spatula,
leaving the seeds in sieve. Pour 1 quart
cold water through sieve to get out
remaining juices. Stir lemonade. Add 1
ounce Smirnoff® Raspberry Flavored
vodka to each glass. Makes 4 drinks.

Haute Hosting

Remember these helpful hints when hosting a party to celebrate responsibly: offer soft drinks, fruit juices, water, or other non-alcoholic drinks, ensure that food is available, don't serve more than one drink at a time to your guests, and if one of your guests has too much to drink, offer to take them home or call a cab.

Getting Started

(1 month ahead for a formal party;
2 weeks ahead for a casual gathering)

__Decide on the date, place, and style of party.

__Make up the guest list.

__Plan the menu.

__For formal parties, mail invitations. For casual parties, mail invitations or telephone your guests to invite them.

__Decide what table settings, decorations, center-pieces, and music you'll use.

__Make arrangements for any items you'll need to rent or borrow.

Preliminary Preparations

(1 to 2 weeks ahead)

__Telephone any guests who have not responded to your invitations so you can get a definite guest count.

__Do preliminary housecleaning, especially any time-consuming tasks. Make sure all appliances that you'll be using work.

__Compile your grocery shopping list.

__Check that table linens are clean and ready to go. Decide on tableware and serving pieces.

__Order any special flowers, meats, seafood, or other ingredients you'll need.

__If you're making decorations or centerpieces yourself, now's the time to get started.

__If possible, make some foods ahead and freeze them.

Gearing Up

(2 to 3 days ahead)

__Shop for everything but the most perishable items.

__After you return from shopping, recheck your recipes to make sure you have everything you need.

__Plan your timetable for cooking the foods.

__If possible, make items you can store at room temperature, such as snack mixes, ahead.

Ultra premium spirits for high-end cocktails

Haute Hosting

24 Hours to Go
(1 day ahead)

___Shop for perishable and last-minute items.

___Reclean the house as necessary.

___Decorate for the party. Prepare an area for coats and umbrellas.

___If possible, arrange and set your table(s) and serving areas.

___Prepare as many recipes and ingredients as possible. For example, chop vegetables you'll cook as part of a recipe.

___Thaw frozen items. If the items are perishable, thaw them in the refrigerator.

___Decide on your wardrobe.

Let's Party
(1 hour ahead)

___Put all the finishing touches on the meal and tables.

___Clear a spot for placing used dishes as guests finish with them and provide an easily accessible place for garbage.

___Set out cheese and nonperishable appetizers or snacks, if using.

___Get dressed.

As the Doorbell Rings
(5 to 15 minutes ahead)

___Open wine, if serving. Set out remaining appetizers or snacks, if serving.

___Light candles and turn on music, if using.

___Set out cheese and nonperishable appetizers or snacks, if serving.

___Have a cocktail.

California wines for entertaining

Sparkling Mimosa Combine ¾ ounce Cîroc® vodka, ¾ ounce Sterling Vintner's Collection® chardonnay, ¼ ounce peach schnapps, and 1 ounce Stirrings® Simple Tart cranberry soda in a wine glass. Garnish with a cranberry and mint leaf. Makes 1 drink.

All natural, simple cocktail mixers

EASY
ENTERTAINING
AT HOME

Rio Rum Punch In a punch bowl, combine 3 cups chilled peach nectar, 2 cups frozen peaches, 2 cups chilled Captain Morgan® Original Spiced Rum, 1 cup chilled Stirrings® Simple Peach Bellini, and 2 cups chilled ginger ale. Garnish with peach slices or pineapple spears. Makes 12 servings.

SEPTEMBER

Racecar 500 **Team Spirit**
Scoreboard Sliders **Best**
Hush Puppies Take Me Away
Berry Crumble Florida
Orange **Royal Crown** Pro-
secco Cake **Swamp Water**
Poker Chip **Sorbet Shooters**
Racecar 500 **Team Spirit**
Scoreboard Sliders **Best**
Hush Puppies Take Me Away
Berry Crumble Florida
Orange **Royal Crown** Pro-
secco Cake **Swamp Water**
Poker Chip **Sorbet Shooters**

Fashion Week: Combine 1 bottle Stirrings® Red Sangria Cocktail Mixer with 1 bottle BV Coastal Estates® merlot. Pour into wineglasses. Makes 11 drinks.

RACECAR 500

MAKES: 1 cocktail

1½ ounces Smirnoff® Citrus
     Flavored vodka
3 ounces cranberry juice
1 lime wedge

Fill lowball glass with ice.
Add vodka and cranberry juice.
Stir well. Garnish with lime wedge.

TEAM SPIRIT

MAKES: 1 cocktail

1¼ ounces Tanqueray® London Dry Gin
2 ounces cranberry juice
2 ounces orange juice

In a cocktail shaker half filled with ice,
add gin, cranberry juice, and orange juice.
Shake well and strain into a footed glass
filled with ice.

SCOREBOARD SLIDERS

SERVES: 4

COOK TIME: 20 minutes

FOR THE RED PEPPER KETCHUP:

- ¼ cup ketchup
- 1 (12-ounce) jar roasted red peppers

FOR THE PESTO MAYO:

- ½ cup mayonnaise
- 2 tablespoons pesto

FOR THE BURGERS:

- 2 cups frozen chopped onions
- 5 tablespoons canola oil
- 1½ pounds ground beef, 85 percent lean
- 2 tablespoons grill seasoning
- ¼ pound blue cheese, sliced into 4 pieces
- 2 slices cheddar cheese, each piece cut into 4
- 2 slices mozzarella cheese, each piece cut into 4
- 12 small dinner potato rolls, sliced in half and toasted

TO MAKE RED PEPPER KETCHUP:

In a mini chopper or blender, combine ketchup and roasted red peppers (reserve one red pepper to garnish the burgers). Blend until smooth. Set aside.

TO MAKE PESTO MAYO:

Combine mayonnaise and pesto in a small bowl and stir together. Set aside.

TO MAKE BURGERS:

Heat 3 tablespoons of oil in a large pan over medium-low heat. Add onion and cook until caramelized, about 15 to 20 minutes, making sure to stir every few minutes.

Form the ground beef into 12 equal-sized mini patties. Heat the remaining oil in a large skillet over medium-high heat. Season both sides of each patty with the grill seasoning and place into the skillet. Cook for 3 minutes. Flip the burgers, top four with the blue cheese, the next four with 2 slices of cheddar cheese each, and the final four with 2 slices of mozzarella cheese each. Cover with a lid and cook for another 2 to 3 minutes until cheese is melted.

Place the burgers onto the bottom half of each roll. Top the blue-cheese burgers with the caramelized onion then with the top of the roll. Slice the reserved red pepper into 4 pieces. Top the cheddar burgers with roasted red pepper pieces, roasted red pepper ketchup, and the top of the roll. Finally, top the mozzarella burgers with the pesto mayo and the top half of the roll.

BEST HUSH PUPPIES

MAKES: 24 hush puppies
COOK TIME: 20 minutes

FOR THE HUSH PUPPIES:

- 1 (8.5-ounce) box corn bread or muffin mix
- ¼ cup cornmeal
- ¼ cup chopped onions
- 1 egg
- ½ cup sweet potato puree
  About 4 strips crumbled bacon
  Vegetable oil for frying

Fill a medium heavy-bottomed pot with enough oil to come ⅓ of the way up the side. Place over medium heat.

In a large bowl, mix together all ingredients for hush puppies until well combined. When oil reaches 350°F, carefully place batter by the heaping tablespoonful into oil, using two spoons. Fry in batches until golden brown and cooked through, about 3 to 4 minutes. Remove from oil and place onto a tray lined with paper towels to drain. Serve immediately, with Honey Mustard dip on the side.

TAKE ME AWAY

SERVES: 2

2   ounces pink grapefruit juice
1   ounce Smirnoff® Vanilla
    Flavored vodka
1   ounce Campari
1   ounce Stirrings® club soda
    Grapefruit wedge, for garnish

Add all ingredients to a highball glass filled with ice and stir. Garnish with grapefruit wedge.

BERRY CRUMBLE

MAKES: 8 slices
COOK TIME: 50 minutes

3   (12-ounce) bags frozen mixed berries,
     thawed
     Zest and juice of 1 lemon
1   cup sugar
3   tablespoons instant tapioca
1   premade deep-dish frozen piecrust
¾   cup flour
¾   cup packed brown sugar
4   tablespoons cold butter, cubed
1   cup granola
1   (8-ounce) container whipped topping
2   tablespoons maple syrup

Preheat oven to 375°F. Place rack in the bottom third of the oven. Put piecrust on a baking sheet lined with parchment paper.

In a large bowl, combine the berries with lemon zest, juice, sugar, and tapioca. Stir together to completely combine. Set aside.

In a medium bowl, mix together the flour and brown sugar. Using a fork or a pastry cutter, cut in the butter until mixture resembles coarse crumbs. Mix in the granola.

Pour berry mixture into piecrust and top with granola crumb topping. Bake for about 45 to 50 minutes or until top of pie is golden brown. Remove from oven and cool at least 1 hour on a wire cooling rack before serving.

Combine whipped topping and maple syrup and mix until well blended. Serve over pie.

FLORIDA ORANGE

SERVES: 4

- 4   orange slices, plus more for garnish
- 2   tablespoons sugar
- 2   tablespoons syrup from a jar of maraschino cherries
- 4   dashes Stirrings® Blood Orange bitters
- 4   ounces Bulleit® bourbon
- 1   bottle (6.3 fluid ounces) Stirrings® club soda

In a pitcher, combine the orange slices and sugar. Muddle with the back of a wooden spoon or a muddler until the sugar is dissolved and juice is extracted from oranges. Add the syrup, bitters, and bourbon and mix well. Pour into 4 lowball glasses filled with ice, top each with club soda, and garnish with an orange slice.

ROYAL CROWN

MAKES: 1 cocktail

1½   ounces Crown Royal® Deluxe whisky

6   ounces club soda

Add whisky to an ice-filled highball glass, top with club soda, and stir.

PROSECCO CAKE

SERVES: 8

COOK TIME: 50 minutes

FOR THE CAKES:

1   (16-ounce) box pound cake mix

2   eggs

½   stick butter, softened

1   teaspoon orange zest

⅓   cup Stellina di Notte® Prosecco or sparkling wine

⅓   cup orange juice

1½   cups confectioners' sugar

¼   cup sparkling wine

Preheat oven to 350°F. Spray two 9 × 5-inch loaf pans with nonstick cooking spray and dust lightly with flour.

In a large mixing bowl, combine all ingredients for cake. Mix on medium speed until well incorporated. Pour into prepared loaf pans. Bake for 40 to 50 minutes or until top is golden brown. Allow to cool for 5 minutes then remove from pans and cool completely on a wire rack placed on a sheet pan.

To make glaze, put confectioners' sugar in a large bowl and slowly beat in the Prosecco until consistency is thick but pourable. Pour glaze over top of cakes and allow to drip down sides. Let sit for 5 minutes to set.

SWAMP WATER

MAKES: 1 cocktail

4 ounces lime drink

1 ounce apricot brandy

1 ounce Smirnoff® Citrus
Flavored vodka

Splash Stirrings® Clarified
Key Lime juice

In a shaker, mix all ingredients.
Pour into highball glass
filled with ice.

POKER CHIP

MAKES: 1 cocktail

1½   ounces Captain Morgan Parrot Bay®
     Coconut rum

5   fresh mint leaves, torn

½   ounce cream of coconut

     Splash Stirrings® Clarified
     Key Lime juice

     Stirrings® club soda

     Ice cubes

     Fresh mint sprigs, for garnish

Add the rum, mint leaves, cream of
coconut, and lime juice to a cocktail
shaker filled with ice cubes. Shake
several times and strain into a chilled
highball glass. Top with club soda and
garnish with a sprig of mint.

SORBET SHOOTERS

MAKES: 10 cocktails

1 pint lemon, orange, or raspberry sorbet

¾ cup lemon, orange, or raspberry
flavored liqueur

Using a melon baller, place small scoops of sorbet into each chilled shot glass (only 1 flavor per glass). Top sorbet with about 1 tablespoon of matching flavored liqueur. Serve immediately.

OCTOBER

Bacon Bites Crispy Fritters
Cinnamon Rum Cider
Autumn Sunset Pumpkin
Pie Witches' Brew A Crys-
tal Ball Skull and Bone
Fairies' Cheesecake Fairy
Queen Buttered Apple
Orange Tiramisu Bacon
Bites Crispy Fritters
Cinnamon Rum Cider
Autumn Sunset Pumpkin
Pie Witches' Brew A Crys-
tal Ball Skull and Bone

Witch's Broomstick: Add 1½ ounces Jose Cuervo® Especial Gold tequila, 1½ ounces Jose Cuervo® Lime Margarita Mix, 1½ ounces mango juice, 1 cup diced and peeled mangos, and 4 ounces crushed ice to a blender, and blend until smooth. Pour into a glass. Garnish with a mango wedge. Makes 1 drink.

BACON BITES

SERVES: 6

COOK TIME: 25 minutes

½ pound thick-cut bacon

½ cup chopped pecans

½ cup brown sugar

4 slices rye bread

½ cup cream cheese, softened

1 tablespoon Worcestershire sauce

2 tablespoons chopped chives

Black pepper, to taste

Preheat the oven to 375°F.

Line a baking sheet with aluminum foil and top it with a baking rack. Place the bacon in one layer on top of the rack.

Mix together the pecans and brown sugar with black pepper. Sprinkle the mixture evenly over the bacon. Put the bacon into the oven and bake until the sugar is melted and the bacon is crisp, about 25 minutes. Remove and let cool a bit until crisp.

While the bacon is cooking, toast the bread and cut into quarters. Mix together the cream cheese and Worcestershire sauce.

To serve, spread the toast with the cream cheese mixture and top with a piece or two of bacon cut to fit. Then top with another dollop of the cream cheese mixture and garnish with chopped chives.

CRISPY FRITTERS

SERVES: 4

COOK TIME: 15 minutes

1 (8.5-ounce) box corn muffin mix

1 (8-ounce) can creamed corn

1 egg, lightly beaten

¾ cup shredded mozzarella cheese

½ cup canola oil

2 tablespoons pesto

1 cup grape tomatoes, halved

Salt, to taste

Black pepper, to taste

In a medium bowl, add corn muffin mix, creamed corn, egg, and ¼ cup mozzarella cheese. Mix until combined.

Heat ¼ cup oil in a nonstick skillet over medium heat. Working in batches, spoon the batter into the hot oil by heaping tablespoonfuls. Cook about 2 to 3 minutes per side until crisp and golden brown.

In a medium bowl, combine 2 tablespoons of the pesto with ½ cup shredded cheese, and season with salt. Place a tablespoon of the pesto and cheese onto each of the corn fritters, and top each with a tomato half. Transfer to a platter and serve.

CINNAMON RUM CIDER

MAKES: 4 cocktails

3   cups apple cider

4   cinnamon sticks

½   cup Captain Morgan® Original Spiced rum

2   ounces Goldschläger® cinnamon schnapps

8   kumquats, for garnish

In a 4-quart slow cooker, combine apple cider, cinnamon sticks, rum, and schnapps. Cover, and cook at high-heat setting for 1 hour. Ladle into glass mugs. Slice kumquats in half. Cut 2 wooden skewers in half. Thread each skewer half with 4 kumquat slices, and use for garnish.

AUTUMN SUNSET

MAKES: 2 cocktails

1½ ounces Smirnoff® Cherry Flavored vodka

1½ ounces plum wine

Ice cubes

Plums, sliced, for garnish

In a cocktail shaker filled with ice cubes, add vodka and plum wine. Shake. Strain into chilled martini glasses. Garnish with plum slices.

PUMPKIN PIE

SERVES: 8
COOK TIME: 5 minutes

½ cup sugar
½ teaspoon pumpkin pie spice
1½ cups Smirnoff® Vanilla Flavored vodka
Stirrings® Tart Cranberry flavored
sparkling water

In a small pot over medium heat, mix together the sugar and pumpkin pie spice with ½ cup water. Bring to a boil and remove from heat. Allow to cool and strain through cheesecloth into jar.

Fill a pitcher with ice and add the vodka and half the sugar-and-spice syrup. (Add more syrup to taste.) Stir until cold. Strain evenly into chilled martini glasses and top with sparkling water.

WITCHES' BREW

MAKES: 2 cocktails

- ½   cup orange soda
- 1   cup orange juice
- 1   ounce Stirrings® triple sec
- 2   ounces Smirnoff No. 21™ vodka
- 1   peppermint stick
- 1   licorice wheel

In a small pitcher, combine the orange soda, orange juice, triple sec, and vodka. Divide evenly between two martini glasses. Garnish with peppermint stick or licorice wheel.

A CRYSTAL BALL

MAKES: 3 cocktails

- 2   cups Ocean Spray white cranberry juice
- 2   ounces Smirnoff® Green Apple Flavored vodka
- 2   ounces Goldschläger® cinnamon schnapps
- 3   ice balls

Use 3 silicone ice ball molds (available at www.muji.com) to make 3 ice balls according to manufacturer's instructions.

Combine juice, vodka, and schnapps in a pitcher and stir together. Place the ice balls into 3 chilled martini glasses and evenly divide the cocktail between the glasses.

SKULL AND BONE

MAKES: 1 cocktail

1¼ ounces Crown Royal® Deluxe whisky

¼ ounce amaretto liqueur

6 ounces cranberry juice

1 tube red candy gel

4 gummy vampire teeth

Add whisky, amaretto liqueur, and
cranberry juice in a flute glass and stir.
Garnish with red candy gel and gummy
vampire teeth.

FAIRIES' CHEESECAKE

SERVES: 8

1 store-bought frozen cheesecake
1 cup white chocolate chips
2 tablespoons white sprinkles
2 tablespoons edible white sugar pearls
2 tablespoons silver dragées
2 tablespoons white edible glitter
8 ice pop sticks

Warm a knife under hot water and cut the cheesecake into 8 slices. To ensure clean slices, make sure to wipe off the blade and place it under hot water before cutting each slice.

Insert a stick halfway into the back end of each slice. Place cheesecake slices in freezer for 1–2 hours until frozen.
Put chocolate chips in a bowl and place bowl over a pot of simmering water. Stir frequently until chips melt.

Place the cheesecake slices onto a baking sheet fitted with a piece of parchment paper. Drizzle each slice with the melted white chocolate. Sprinkle each slice with a decoration. Return to freezer for about 5 minutes until chocolate is set. Place on a platter and serve.

FAIRY QUEEN

MAKES: 3 cocktails

3   ounces half and half
3   ounces Smirnoff® Vanilla
     Flavored vodka
3   ounces Godiva® White
     Chocolate liqueur
¾   ounce hazelnut liqueur
3   white long-stemmed feathers

In a pitcher filled with ice, combine half
and half, vodka, white chocolate liqueur,
and hazelnut liqueur. Mix together and
pour into chilled tall, footed glasses.
Garnish with a feather.

BUTTERED APPLE

SERVES: 6
COOK TIME: 1 hour

1   stick butter, softened
¼   cup light brown sugar
½   teaspoon ground nutmeg
½   teaspoon ground cinnamon
½   teaspoon ground cloves
3   cups apple cider
1   cup Bulleit® bourbon

In a bowl, combine butter, sugar, and spices. Whisk until butter becomes creamy and ingredients are incorporated. Roll butter mixture into 1-inch log. Wrap log in plastic wrap and refrigerate at least 1 hour.

Meanwhile, place apple cider in a 1- to 1½-quart slow cooker. Cover and heat on high-heat setting for 1 hour.

Divide the bourbon equally among 6 glasses. Add hot cider to each glass and top with a slice of spiced butter.

ORANGE TIRAMISU

SERVES: 4

1	teaspoon instant espresso powder
⅓	cup Grand Marnier liqueur
16-24	lady finger cookies
1	(1-ounce) box cheesecake-flavored instant pudding mix
1¾	cups milk
1	teaspoon orange extract
	Cocoa powder, for dusting

In a shallow bowl, stir espresso powder into ⅓ cup warm water until dissolved. Stir in Grand Marnier. Dip lady fingers into espresso mixture and use them to line the sides of 4 parfait glasses. Set aside.

In a large bowl, whisk together pudding mix, milk, and orange extract for 2 minutes. Divide pudding mixture among the glasses. Let sit for 5 minutes. Dust tops with cocoa powder and serve.

NOVEMBER

Sweet Crostata Lovely
Lady Spiced Orange
Golden Tarts Copper Ket
tle Cider Cake Lorraine
Sandy's Spiced Wine Per
fect Cocoa Maple Cakes
Golden Glory Golden
Cupcakes Lovely Martin
Pear Puffs Dim All the
Lights Born This Way
Sweet Crostata Lovely
Lady Spiced Orange
Golden Tarts Copper Ket
tle Cider Cake Lorraine

Hot Coffee Cocktail: Pour 1 ounce Jose Cuervo® Especial Gold tequila and 1 ounce Godiva® Mocha liqueur into a glass mug. Fill mug with 2 ounces hot coffee. Top with a dollop whipped cream. Makes 1 drink.

SWEET CROSTATA

SERVES: 6 to 8

COOK TIME: 18 minutes

1   premade piecrust

2   teaspoons citrus herb seasoning

4   ounces cream cheese, softened

½   (10-ounce) jar fig preserves

1   (3-ounce) package proscuitto,
    cut into ½-inch strips

1   egg

Preheat oven to 425°F.

Place the piecrust on a baking sheet.
Spread cream cheese over piecrust, leaving
a 1-inch border. Sprinkle with the citrus
herb seasoning. Top with fig preserves.
Fold piecrust border over fig spread. Top
with prosciutto strips.

Lightly beat egg with one tablespoon of
water, and use a pastry brush to brush edge
of crust with egg wash. Bake in oven for 15
to 18 minutes. Let cool 5 minutes.

LOVELY LADY

MAKES: 2 cocktails

1½ ounces apple brandy

2 ounces Stirrings® triple sec

1½ cups orange juice

In a shaker, combine all ingredients. Stir and strain into chilled martini glasses.

SPICED ORANGE

MAKES: 8 drinks

COOK TIME: 10 minutes

3   cups apple cider

2   cups orange juice

1   cup cranberry juice cocktail

1   cup Captain Morgan® Original
    Spiced rum

1   teaspoon pumpkin pie spice

½   cup dark brown sugar

1   orange, sliced

1   cinnamon stick

2   cups whipped topping

Combine all ingredients except whipped topping in a large pot. Heat on medium low for 10 minutes. Serve in heatproof mugs or glasses. Place a dollop of whipped topping on top.

GOLDEN TARTS

SERVES: 4

COOK TIME: 32 minutes

2 tablespoons extra-virgin olive oil

1 tablespoon unsalted butter

1½ cups chopped onions

1 tablespoon sugar

4 ounces goat cheese, softened

1 large egg

2 tablespoons heavy cream

1 teaspoon fresh thyme leaves

1 (14-ounce) box refrigerated piecrust

Salt, to taste

In a large heavy-bottomed skillet over medium heat, add the oil and butter. When the butter is melted, add the onions, sugar, and salt to taste. Cook until the onions begin to brown. Turn the heat to low and cook slowly, turning often, until the onions are golden brown and caramelized, about 12 minutes. Remove from the heat and set aside to cool.

Preheat the oven to 375°F.

In a bowl, mix together the goat cheese, egg, cream, and thyme. Pour mixture into a plastic food-storage bag. Snip off a corner of the bag to use it for piping.

Lay a piecrust out flat, and with a 2½-inch round cutter cut out 12 circles. Press them into the cups of a 12-count nonstick mini-muffin tin. Fill each cup halfway with the cooled onions. Pipe the cheese mixture on top of the onions, filling up the cups. Bake the tarts until the filling is set, about 15 to 20 minutes. Let cool, then remove them from the muffin tin and serve.

COPPER KETTLE CIDER

MAKES: 1 drink

1½   ounces Crown Royal® Deluxe whisky

2   ounces heated cider

¼   ounce honey

¼   ounce lemon juice

1   sprinkle cinnamon

Put whisky, warm cider, and lemon juice in a
coffee mug. Add honey and stir. Sprinkle
cinnamon on top.

SPICED COFFEE CAKE

SERVES: 10

COOK TIME: 6 hours

Butter-flavored cooking spray

1 (16-ounce) box pound cake mix

¾ cup cinnamon applesauce

⅓ cup pasteurized packaged egg whites

1 teaspoon pumpkin pie spice

½ teaspoon almond extract

¼ cup baking mix, Bisquick®

2 tablespoons brown sugar

¾ cup chopped walnuts

1 (0.74-ounce) packet spiced cider drink mix, Alpine®

1 tablespoon butter, melted

Whipped topping flavored with vanilla extract, for serving

Lightly spray a 6-cup soufflé dish with cooking spray and set aside. Make a foil ring ½-inch thick for soufflé dish to sit on and place inside the bottom of a 5-quart slow cooker.

In a large bowl, combine cake mix, applesauce, eggs, pumpkin pie spice, and almond extract. Using an electric mixer, beat on low speed for 30 seconds. Scrape down sides of bowl and beat for 1 minute on medium speed. Pour into soufflé dish and set aside.

In a medium bowl, stir together baking mix, brown sugar, walnuts, cider mix, and melted butter. Sprinkle over cake batter. Use a butter knife to cut through cake and topping to swirl.

Place soufflé dish on top of foil ring in slow cooker. Place 5 folded paper towels over slow cooker bowl and secure with lid. Cook on LOW setting for 4 to 6 hours or until tester comes out clean. Do not lift lid to check cake for the first 3 hours.

Cool in soufflé dish on wire rack for 15 to 20 minutes before removing and slicing. Serve with whipped topping.

SANDY'S SPICED WINE

MAKES: 10 cocktails
COOK TIME: 5 minutes

2 bottles red wine, BV Coastal Estates®
Cabernet Sauvignon

2 tablespoons light brown sugar

1½ teaspoons pumpkin pie spice

¼ cup raisins

2 oranges, sliced, for garnish

10 cinnamon sticks, for garnish

Combine all ingredients in a large pot.
Bring to simmer over medium-low heat,
remove from heat, and let steep for
5 minutes. Garnish with cinnamon stick
and orange slice. Serve hot.

PERFECT COCOA

MAKES: 8 drinks

COOK TIME: 8 minutes

6   (12-ounce) cans evaporated milk

1   cup sugar

¾   cup cocoa powder, plus more for garnish

1   teaspoon nutmeg

⅔   cup Baileys® Coffee liqueur

⅔   cup Captain Morgan Parrot Bay® Coconut rum

Whipped topping, for serving

In a large pot, whisk together milk, sugar, cocoa, nutmeg, coffee liqueur, and coconut rum. Heat to a simmer over low heat, whisking occasionally. Let simmer for 2 minutes. Serve with whipped topping and a dusting of cocoa powder.

MAPLE CAKES

MAKES: 12 cakes

COOK TIME: 12 minutes

FOR THE CAKES:

1   egg

½   cup maple syrup

½   cup heavy cream

1   teaspoon vanilla extract

2   cups baking mix, Bisquick®

⅓   cup chopped walnuts

FOR THE GLAZE:

1   cup confectioners' sugar

1   teaspoon pumpkin pie spice

1   tablespoon maple syrup

¼   cup heavy cream

12   walnut halves, for garnish

Preheat oven to 350°F. Line a 12-cup muffin tin with paper liners.

In a medium bowl, beat together egg, maple syrup, heavy cream, and vanilla extract. In a large bowl put baking mix. Add wet ingredients to the baking mix and beat until well incorporated, about 1 minute. Gently stir in chopped walnuts. Fill muffin tins about two-thirds full. Bake until golden brown, about 10 to 12 minutes. Cool before removing from pan and cooling completely on a wire rack.

TO MAKE GLAZE:

Stir together confectioners' sugar with pumpkin pie spice, maple syrup, and heavy cream.

Whisk slowly until a thick but pourable consistency is reached. Dip cakes into the icing bowl to coat the top, and garnish each with a walnut half.

GOLDEN GLORY

MAKES: 6 cocktails

- 1 bottle sparkling cider
- 4 ounces Goldschläger® cinnamon schnapps
- 4 ounces Smirnoff® Vanilla Flavored vodka
- 1 (12-ounce) can Stirrings® ginger ale, chilled

Fill 4 chilled champagne saucers halfway with the sparkling cider. Add an ounce of cinnamon schnapps and an ounce of vanilla vodka to each glass. Top with a splash of ginger ale and serve.

GOLDEN CUPCAKES

MAKES: 24 cupcakes
COOK TIME: 12 minutes

FOR THE CUPCAKES:
- 1 (18.25-ounce) box golden butter cake mix
- 3 eggs
- 1 stick butter, softened
- 1¼ cups milk
- ½ (13.4-ounce) can dulce de leche
  Gold dragées for decorating

FOR THE FROSTING:
- 2 cups heavy cream
- 1½ cans dulce de leche

TO MAKE CUPCAKES:

Preheat oven to 350°F. Line two 12-cup muffin tins with gold foil liners.

In a large mixing bowl, combine the cake mix with eggs, butter, and milk. Using a hand mixer, beat on medium speed for 2 minutes, until well incorporated. In a small bowl, mix together the ½ can of dulce de leche with 1 cup of cake batter and set aside. Fill muffin tins halfway with the batter. Spoon a tablespoon of dulce de leche mixture into each cupcake liner and swirl it into batter with a butter knife. Bake for 10 to 12 minutes or until tops are golden brown. Remove from oven and cool in tins before cooling completely on a wire rack.

TO MAKE FROSTING:

In a mixing bowl, beat 2 cups of cold heavy cream until just before soft peaks form. Add the dulce de leche and beat until soft peaks form. Frost each cupcake with the caramel frosting and sprinkle with gold dragées.

LOVELY MARTINI

MAKES: 2 cocktails

- 2 ounces Baileys® Irish cream liqueur
- 3 ounces Godiva® Chocolate liqueur
- 1 ounce hazelnut liqueur
- 1 ounce half and half
- Ice
- 1 chocolate-covered candy bar stick, chopped

Fill a cocktail shaker with ice. Pour Irish cream, chocolate liqueur, hazelnut liqueur, and half and half over ice. Shake vigorously; strain into 2 chilled martini glasses. Garnish with chopped candy bar stick.

PEAR PUFFS

MAKES: 16 puffs
COOK TIME: 20 minutes

- 1 egg
- 1 sheet frozen puff pastry, thawed
- 5 tablespoons, plus 1 teaspoon, semisoft cheese with garlic and fine herbs
- ⅔ cup diced pears, drained and thinly sliced

Preheat oven to 400°F. Line 2 baking sheets with parchment paper and set aside. For egg wash, in a small bowl, lightly whisk together egg and 1 teaspoon water. Set aside.

Unroll puff pastry sheet on a lightly floured surface. Using a rolling pin, roll puff pastry into a 14 × 10-inch rectangle. Cut into sixteen 3½ × 2½-inch rectangles.

Spread 1 teaspoon of the semisoft cheese in middle of a pastry rectangle. Top with 2 teaspoons of the pears. Using a pastry brush, brush egg wash around perimeter of the puff pastry rectangle. Bring corners of the pastry to the center and pinch seams together. Repeat to make 16 puffs. Arrange puffs, seam sides up, on prepared baking sheets. Refrigerate for 15 minutes. Remove from refrigerator and brush tops with remaining egg wash.

Bake for 20 to 25 minutes or until puffed and golden brown. Remove from oven and cool for 5 minutes. Serve warm.

DIM ALL THE LIGHTS

SERVES: 16

4   cups cranberry juice cocktail,
    Ocean Spray
2   cups Smirnoff No. 21™ vodka
1   cup cherry brandy
4   cups cola
    Maraschino cherries

In a punch bowl, combine cranberry juice cocktail, vodka, and cherry brandy. Slowly add cola. Serve over ice in lowball glasses. Garnish with maraschino cherries.

BORN THIS WAY

MAKES: 4 cocktails

    Ice
½ cup frozen raspberries
¼ cup frozen limeade concentrate,
    Minute Maid
4 ounces Jose Cuervo® Silver tequila
2 ounces Grand Marnier orange liqueur
2 ounces cranberry juice cocktail

Fill a blender with ice. Add raspberries,
limeade concentrate, tequila, Grand Marnier,
and cranberry juice cocktail, blend until
slushy. Pour into 4 margarita glasses.

DECEMBER

New York Martini Mix 1½ ounces Cîroc®
vodka and 1½ ounces lemon juice.
Shake with crushed ice. Strain into a
champagne flute rimmed with ½ ounce
simple syrup and ½ teaspoon sugar. Fill
with crushed ice. Makes 1 drink.

TIRAMISU CRÈME WITH ESPRESSO

SERVES: 4

1 (8-ounce) container whipped topping

1 cup mascarpone cheese, at room temperature

1 tablespoon instant espresso powder

2 teaspoons cocoa powder

¼ cup marsala

½ cup confectioners' sugar

½ teaspoon vanilla extract

8 lady finger cookies

Additional cocoa powder or chocolate shavings, for garnish

In a large bowl, using a stand mixer, beat together the whipped topping with mascarpone cheese until light and fluffy.

In another small bowl, stir together the espresso powder and cocoa with marsala, vanilla, and sugar. Beat this coffee syrup into whipped topping and cheese mixture.

Spoon into four dessert glasses and refrigerate. Garnish with two lady finger cookies and cocoa powder.

FROZEN HOT COCOA

MAKES: 4 cocktails

- 4 ounces hot cocoa mix, divided use
- 3 cups milk
- ¾ cup Smirnoff® Vanilla Flavored vodka
- ¼ cup mini marshmallows, for garnish

Put 1 ounce cocoa mix onto saucer. Put some water onto another saucer. Dip the rims of 4 martini glasses into the water and shake off any excess. Dip the glasses in the cocoa mix.

In a blender, combine remaining cocoa mix, milk, vodka, and 6 cups ice and blend until smooth. Divide the mixture among the prepared glasses and garnish with the marshmallows and cocoa mix.

ANGEL CAKES

MAKES: 12 cakes
COOK TIME: 22 minutes

FOR THE CAKE:

½   (16-ounce) box angel food cake mix

⅔   cup coconut water

FOR THE FROSTING:

2   egg whites

1   cup sugar

1   tablespoon light corn syrup

¼   teaspoon cream of tartar

¼   cup marshmallow cream

½   cup coconut flakes, for decorating

Preheat oven to 350°F.

Beat together cake mix with coconut water. Fill two 6-count mini angel-food cake pans halfway with batter. Bake for 12 to 15 minutes or until golden brown. Cool completely before removing cakes from pans.

In a medium saucepan, bring 2 cups of water to a simmer.

In a large glass bowl that will fit over saucepan of boiling water, combine ¼ cup water, sugar, corn syrup, cream of tartar, and egg whites. Place on top of pot and beat for 7 minutes using an electric hand mixer. Frosting will be smooth and shiny and will form peaks when mixer is lifted from bowl. Remove from heat and slowly beat in marshmallow cream.

Frost each cake with the icing and sprinkle tops with coconut flakes.

AN ASPEN HOLIDAY

MAKES: 1 cocktail

1¼ ounces Captain Morgan Parrot Bay® Coconut rum

1 ounce milk

5 ounces pineapple juice

Combine rum, milk, and pineapple juice in a blender. Blend 10 to 15 seconds and pour into a tall flute glass.

GOAT CHEESE ROLL

SERVES: 8

COOK TIME: 10 minutes

½ cup olive oil

½ teaspoon red pepper flakes

2 teaspoons garlic, chopped

2 tablespoons butter

½ cup macadamia nuts, chopped

½ cup panko bread crumbs

½ teaspoon white pepper

2 (8-ounce) logs goat cheese

1 (5.25-ounce) box Melba toast

Salt, to taste

Heat the olive oil in a small pot over medium-low heat until the oil is hot but not over 230°F. Remove from heat. Add red pepper flakes and garlic and set aside to cool and let the flavors infuse into the oil. Reserve 2 tablespoons for coating the Melba toasts.

Melt butter in a large skillet over medium-low heat. Add the macadamia nuts, panko, white pepper, and a generous pinch of salt. Let cook for 4 to 5 minutes, stirring frequently, until the nuts and bread crumbs have absorbed all the butter and are lightly toasted. Transfer to a baking sheet and let cool. Once cooled, roll the goat cheese logs in the mixture until they are completely coated. Place on a serving platter with Melba toast.

Add Melba toasts to a large bowl. Drizzle over 2 tablespoons of the garlic pepper oil and toss so all the toasts are coated with the oil.

WHITE CHOCOLATE EGGNOG

MAKES: 8 cocktails

1   quart eggnog
½   cup Myers's® Platinum White rum
½   cup Godiva® White Chocolate liqueur
1   cup whipped topping
    Grated white chocolate, for garnish
    Pumpkin pie spice, for garnish

In a large pitcher, combine eggnog, rum, and white chocolate liqueur. Pour the mixture into cups. Place a heaping tablespoon of the whipped topping into each cup. Garnish with the grated white chocolate and a sprinkling of pumpkin pie spice.

COUNTRY CHRISTMAS

SERVES: 10

8 cups boiling water

16 bags chai spice black tea

½ cup Captain Morgan® Original
Spiced rum

½ cup Smirnoff® Vanilla Flavored vodka

2 cinnamon sticks, plus more for serving

2 cups sweetened condensed milk

Splash in some spiced rum, vanilla vodka, and condensed milk and this ancient Indian secret becomes a festive cocktail you can savor anywhere. Garnish with a cinnamon stick.

Pour boiling water into a 4-quart slow cooker. Place tea bags in slow cooker and secure lid, with tea bag tabs hanging outside. Let steep for 10 minutes. Remove tea bags and discard.

Stir in rum and vodka. Add cinnamon sticks. Cover and cook on low setting for 2 hours. Stir in condensed milk and switch to warm setting for serving.

Serve in Irish coffee mugs with cinnamon-stick swizzles.

ENGLISH POPOVERS

MAKES: 6 popovers
COOK TIME: 15 minutes

1   cup flour
1   cup milk
2   eggs
½   teaspoon garlic and peppercorn
    marinade
½   teaspoon salt
6   tablespoons canola oil

Preheat oven to 450°F.

Divide oil between cups of a 6-cup muffin
pan. Place pan in oven for 5 minutes or until
oil is very hot.

In a blender, combine the flour, milk, eggs,
marinade, and salt. Transfer to a measuring
cup to make it easier to pour into the
muffin cups.

Carefully pour batter about one-third the
way up the sides of the muffin cups. Bake
for 15 minutes. The popovers are done
when they have more than tripled in size
and are golden brown and crisp around the
edges. Serve immediately.

WHIMSICAL WASSAIL

MAKES: 16 drinks

6   inches stick cinnamon, broken
12   whole cloves
6   cups water
1   (12-ounce) can frozen cranberry juice
     cocktail concentrate
1   (12-ounce) can frozen raspberry juice
     blend concentrate
1   (12-ounce) can frozen
     apple juice concentrate
1   cup brandy
⅓   cup lemon juice
¼   cup sugar

Cut a 6-inch square from a double thickness of 100% cotton cheesecloth. Place cinnamon and cloves in center of square, bring
up corners, and tie closed with a kitchen
string. In a 4- to 6-quart slow cooker combine water, juice concentrates, brandy,
lemon juice, and sugar. Add the spice bag
to juice mixture. Cover; cook on low heat
setting for 4 to 6 hours. Remove the spice
bag and discard. Ladle into tall glasses.
Garnish each with a cinnamon stick.

BUTTERBALL MARTINI

MAKES: 1 cocktail

1   ounce Smirnoff® Vanilla
    Flavored vodka
3   ounces pineapple juice
    Splash of black raspberry liqueur
    Splash of butterscotch schnapps

In a cocktail shaker with ice cubes, add vodka, pineapple juice, raspberry liqueur, and schnapps. Shake and strain into a chilled martini glass.

DECK THE HALLS DEVILED EGGS

MAKES: 12 pieces
COOK TIME: 15 minutes

1   dozen eggs
¼   cup mayonnaise
1   tablespoon spicy brown mustard
1   teaspoon lemon juice
2   teaspoons sweet pickle relish
1   teaspoon paprika
2   tablespoons chopped chives, fresh
2   tablespoons crumbled bacon, for
    garnish

Place eggs in a large pot and cover with cold water. Bring to a boil, shut off heat, cover, and let sit for 15 minutes. Drain water from pot and fill with cold water to cool eggs. Change water twice so eggs cool quickly.

Peel eggs, slice off the bottom so that eggs will stand upright. Slice the top third off of each (save tops). Carefully remove egg yolks with a small spoon and place them in a medium-size bowl. Break up the egg yolks with a potato masher. Add all remaining ingredients except bacon and chives. Mix until well blended and smooth.

Transfer mixture to a resealable bag, cut off a corner of the bag, and pipe the filling into each egg. Sprinkle each with chopped chives and bacon bits. Place the tops back onto the eggs. Transfer to a platter and serve.

BLUE PEPPERMINT

MAKES: 1 cocktail

      Ice cubes
¾   ounce brandy
½   ounce crème de cacao
½   ounce Rumple Minze® Peppermint
      schnapps
1   ounce heavy cream
      Blue peppermint stick

In a cocktail shaker filled with ice cubes,
stir together all ingredients except peppermint
stick. Avoid shaking. Strain into rocks
glass filled with ice. Garnish with peppermint stick.

MISTLETOE KISS

MAKES: 1 cocktail

1   ounce green crème de menthe
1   ounce white crème de cacao
2   scoops vanilla
    ice cream
    Fresh mint sprig, for garnish

Place crème de menthe, crème de cacao, and ice cream into a blender. Blend until thick and creamy. Pour into a glass. Garnish with a sprig of mint.

CHERRIES JUBILEE

MAKES: 1 cocktail

½ ounce cherry brandy
3½ ounces extra dry champagne
Bing cherry, for garnish

In a chilled champagne flute, add cherry and cherry brandy. Slowly top off with champagne.

SANTA'S SLEIGH MOCHA

MAKES: 1 drink

3 ounces Baileys® Irish cream liqueur
1 cup hot cocoa
Crushed peppermint candy

In a mug, combine liqueur and hot cocoa. Garnish with crushed peppermint candy.

JANUARY

Pepper Steak Skews
Life Is Short Martin
Blushing Sangria Cran-
berry Pizzazz Pom Per-
fection Cosmo Cream
Warm New Year Thai Iced
Tea Delish Brownies
Meringue Marg Coconut
Bites Pepper Steak Skews
Life Is Short Martin
Blushing Sangria Cran-
berry Pizzazz Pom Per-
fection Cosmo Cream
Warm New Year Thai Iced

Cheers! Shake 1 ounce Cîroc® vodka, 1 dash Grand Marnier, 1½ ounces white cranberry juice, and ½ ounce fresh lime juice over ice. Strain into a chilled champagne flute. Top with 1 ounce champagne. Makes 1 drink.

PEPPER STEAK SKEWS

SERVES: 6
COOK TIME: 6 minutes

FOR THE STEAK ROLLS:

- 1 (2-pound) flank steak
- 1 (12-ounce) jar roasted red peppers, sliced in half
- 1 cup shredded pepper jack cheese
- 2 tablespoons steak seasoning
- 1 tablespoon canola oil
- 12 (10-inch) wooden skewers, soaked in water for 30 minutes

FOR THE SPICY YOGURT SAUCE:

- 1 tablespoon Montreal steak seasoning
- 1 cup plain yogurt
- 1 tablespoon hot sauce
- 1 tablespoon Worcestershire sauce
- 1 tablespoon chopped fresh flat-leaf parsley

Preheat grill over medium heat.

Split steak down the center, cutting almost through, until the two halves open flat to resemble a butterfly shape. Cover the steak with plastic and pound it to about ¼-inch thickness. Cut the pounded steak into 4 equal rectangles. Lay out each steak piece so the grain of the meat goes sideways. Sprinkle 1 tablespoon of seasoning over the steak pieces. Lay a piece of the roasted red pepper on each piece of meat. Sprinkle each piece with ¼ cup of cheese.

Starting from the bottom edge and rolling away from you, roll each piece of beef into a tight log. Place two rolls back to back with the seams facing each other and do the same with the other 2 rolls. Skewer each pair of rolls with 6 skewers spaced evenly apart, so that each skewer pierces both rolls and extends a couple of inches beyond. Slice the rolls between the skewers to give 6 pieces, with 2 round rolls on each skewer, like 2 lolli-pops on a stick. Season the rolls with the remaining steak seasoning.

Brush the grill grates with a tablespoon of oil. Grill skewers for 3 minutes per side. Transfer rolls to a large plate and serve with spicy yogurt sauce.

To make Spicy Yogurt Sauce, combine all ingredients in a bowl and mix until blended.

LIFE IS SHORT MARTINI

MAKES: 2 cocktails

1 ounce Smirnoff® Raspberry
   Flavored vodka
½ ounce crème de cassis
½ ounce Disaronno amaretto
2 ounces cold water
   Ice cubes
   Cherry, for garnish
   Juice of 1 lime

Put ice cubes in a cocktail shaker.
Pour in vodka, crème de cassis,
amaretto, and cold water. Squeeze in lime
juice. Shake. Strain into chilled martini
glasses. Garnish with cherry.

BLUSHING SANGRIA

SERVES: 12

1 bottle Sterling Vintner's Collection®
Meritage dry red wine

1 bottle Sterling Vintner's Collection®
Sauvignon Blanc white wine

½ bottle sparkling water

½ cup brandy

2 oranges

1 nectarine

2 cups red grapes, sliced in half

Squeeze the juice from one orange into a large pitcher. Slice the remaining orange and the nectarine and add to the pitcher along with the grapes. Pour in the wines, sparkling water, and brandy. Mix well, refrigerate, and let the flavors blend for at least 1 hour. To serve, pour the sangria into glasses and spoon in fruit.

CRANBERRY PIZZAZZ

MAKES: 18 drinks

8 whole cardamom pods
Stick cinnamon (16 inches total),
broken

12 whole cloves

4 cups dry red wine, Sterling Vineyards®
Reserve Cabernet Sauvignon

35 ounces cold water

1 (12 ounce) can frozen cranberry
juice concentrate

⅓ cup honey
Cranberries and orange slices,
for garnish

Cut a 6-inch square from a double thickness of 100-percent-cotton cheesecloth to use as a spice bag. Pinch cardamom pods to break. Center the cardamom, cinnamon, and cloves on the cheesecloth square, bring up corners, and tie closed with clean kitchen string. In a 3½- to 6-quart slow cooker, combine spice bag, wine, water, frozen juice concentrate, and honey. Cover and cook on low-heat setting for 4 to 6 hours or on high-heat setting for 2 to 2½ hours. Remove and discard spice bag. Ladle into heatproof glasses and garnish with cranberry and orange slice on a toothpick.

COSMO CREAM

MAKES: 1 cocktail

1½ ounces Smirnoff® Raspberry
     Flavored vodka

3 ounces cranberry juice

¼ ounce orange juice

1 maraschino cherry

Fill chilled martini glass with ice. Add vodka, cranberry juice, and orange juice. Stir well. Garnish with the maraschino cherry.

POM PERFECTION

MAKES: 4 cocktails

1 cup Smirnoff® Pomegranate Martini

1 cup vanilla yogurt
     Ice cubes

To the jar of a blender, add the martini, yogurt, and a cup of ice. Blend until smooth. Pour into chilled tall glasses.

WARM NEW YEAR

SERVES: 4

COOK TIME: 5 minutes

3   cups half and half

4   (1-ounce) envelopes hot cocoa mix

1   tablespoon instant coffee

½   cup Baileys® Coffee liqueur

2   cups whipped topping

    Chocolate shavings, for garnish

In a medium pot over medium heat, warm the half and half until it is steaming. Avoid letting it boil. Whisk in the cocoa mix, instant coffee, and coffee liqueur.

Serve the cocoa in mugs, dolloped with whipped cream and garnished with chocolate shavings.

DELISH BROWNIES

MAKES: 16 brownies
COOK TIME: 35 minutes

- 1 (19.5-ounce) box chocolate brownie mix
- 2 eggs
- ¼ cup chocolate milk
- ¼ cup canola oil
- 1 cup chocolate chips, divided use
- 30 caramels
- ½ cup heavy cream
- 2 cups shredded coconut, toasted

Preheat oven to 350°F and spray a 9 × 13-inch baking dish with cooking spray.

In a large bowl, beat together brownie mix with eggs, chocolate milk, and oil until just combined. Using a spatula, fold in ½ cup chocolate chips. Spread into prepared baking dish and bake for 25 to 30 minutes or until center is barely set. Remove from oven and cool completely.

To make topping, heat cream in a small saucepan over medium-low heat. Stir in caramels until melted and incorporated into the cream. Remove from heat and stir in coconut. Spread in an even layer over cooled brownies.

Melt remaining chocolate chips in microwave at 15-second intervals, stirring between intervals until melted. Drizzle chocolate in a crisscross pattern over coconut topping. Place in the refrigerator for at least 30 minutes to set before slicing into bars.

THAI ICED TEA

MAKES: 2 cocktails

1 (16-ounce) bottle unsweetened
iced tea

¼ cup vanilla chai latte mix, Pacific Chai

¼ cup sweetened condensed milk

8 drops yellow food coloring

4 drops red food coloring

6 ounces Baileys® Irish cream liqueur
Ice cubes
Heavy cream

In a microwave-safe bowl, heat tea in microwave oven on high 3 minutes, until hot.

Add chai latte mix to the hot tea, and stir until dissolved. Stir in condensed milk and food colorings; cool to room temperature. Measure liqueur and stir into the tea mixture.

Fill highball glasses with ice cubes, and then three-quarters full with tea mixture. Carefully pour heavy cream into the glasses over the back of a spoon.

MERINGUE MARG

MAKES: 1 cocktail

1½	ounces Jose Cuervo® Light Margarita
4	ounces crushed ice
1	teaspoon meringue cookie crumbs
1	fresh lime wedge

Mix Jose Cuervo and ice in a blender. Rub the rim of a chilled margarita glass with lime and then dip into crushed meringues. Pour into the glass and garnish with lime wedge.

COCONUT BITES

MAKES: 18 bites

2	tablespoons powdered sugar
2	cups sweetened flaked coconut
1	cup dried apricots, finely chopped
½	cup nut topping
⅔	cup sweetened condensed milk

Sift powdered sugar into a pie plate and set aside.

In a large bowl, mix together coconut, apricots, and nut topping. Add sweetened condensed milk and stir until well mixed.

Scoop a heaping tablespoon of coconut mixture and form into a ball. Roll ball in powdered sugar, coating entire ball. Place ball on ungreased baking sheet. Repeat with the remaining coconut mixture and powdered sugar.

Let stand at room temperature for 1 hour to set.

FEBRUARY

A Swiss Alp Tall, Dark, & Handsome Milk Choco late Cupcakes Choco Martini Lovely Mousse Egg Cream Cocktail Cof fee Cream Cocktail Laven dertini Coconut Rice Pudding Manhattan Man Whiskey A Go Go I Love You Sandra 75 A Swiss Alp Tall, Dark, & Handsome Milk Chocolate Cupcakes Choco Martini Lovely Mousse Egg Cream Cockta

XOXO Cocktail: Drop 2 large ice cubes into a blender. Add 2 ounces Baileys® Original Irish Cream, and 1½ ounces vodka. Blend until completely smooth. Mix in ¼ cup dark chocolate chips. Pour into a tall glass over ice and top with a dollop of whipped cream. Makes 1 drink.

A SWISS ALP

MAKES: 1 cocktail

1 ounce Godiva® Chocolate liqueur
¼ ounce Cîroc® vodka
Dark chocolate shavings

In a chilled martini glass, add chocolate liqueur and vodka. Stir and garnish with chocolate shavings.

TALL, DARK, & HANDSOME

MAKES: 1 cocktail

¼ cup granulated sugar, for rim of glass

1¼ ounces Smirnoff® Vanilla
Flavored vodka

½ ounce Baileys® Coffee liqueur

½ ounce Godiva® Chocolate liqueur

Wet rim of a martini glass on a damp paper towel and dip rim into sugar. Set aside. Add liquid ingredients to a cocktail shaker filled with ice. Stir and strain into the martini glass.

MILK CHOCOLATE CUPCAKES

MAKES: 24 cupcakes
COOK TIME: 12 minutes

1 (18.25-ounce) box milk chocolate cake mix

3 eggs

⅓ cup canola or vegetable oil

1¼ cups chocolate milk

1 (12-ounce) bag semi-sweet chocolate chips, divided use

½ cup heavy cream

Small silver dragées, for decorating

TO MAKE CUPCAKES:

Heat oven to 350°F. Line two 12-cup cupcake tins with silver-foil paper liners.

In a large mixing bowl, combine the eggs, cake mix, oil, and chocolate milk. Beat on medium speed for 2 minutes, scraping until batter is well incorporated.

In a microwave, melt ½ cup of the chocolate chips, stopping to stir at 10-second intervals. Add 1 cup of batter to the melted chocolate and stir well to combine. Place into a resealable plastic bag and snip off one of the bottom corners.

Fill each cupcake liner with 1 small scoop of cake batter, to about a quarter of the way up the cupcake paper. Pipe 1 tablespoon batter with melted chocolate from the plastic bag into each batter-filled cup. Top each with another scoop of the remaining cake batter.

Bake 12 minutes. Remove from oven, allow to cool 1 minute before removing and cooling completely.

TO MAKE DARK CHOCOLATE ICING:

Heat cream in a saucepan over low heat to a simmer. Remove from heat and stir in remaining chocolate chips until completely combined. While still slightly warm, dip the tops of cupcakes in the chocolate icing. Sprinkle with dragées, and allow icing to set.

CHOCO MARTINI

MAKES: 1 cocktail

1 ounce Baileys® Irish cream liqueur
½ ounce Smirnoff No. 21™ vodka
1 ounce espresso

In a cocktail shaker filled with ice, add espresso, vodka, and Irish cream. Shake and strain into a martini glass.

LOVELY MOUSSE

SERVES: 6

1½ cups whipping cream
1 (1.4-ounce) box instant chocolate pudding
2 tablespoons Grand Marnier orange liqueur
2 (3.5-ounce) containers chocolate pudding cups
6 ounces fresh strawberries

In a medium mixing bowl, beat together cream and pudding mix with an electric mixer until soft peaks form.

Add Grand Marnier and pudding cups and beat until stiff. Transfer to a large plastic resealable bag. Snip off one of the bottom corners and pipe mixture into martini glasses.

Serve garnished with fresh strawberries.

EGG CREAM
COCKTAIL

MAKES: 1 cocktail

2   tablespoons chocolate syrup

3   ounces Godiva® Chocolate liqueur

¾   cup milk

¾   cup seltzer

In a 12-ounce glass with ice, stir together
chocolate syrup, chocolate liqueur, and milk.
Top with seltzer and stir. Serve immediately.

COFFEE CREAM COCKTAIL

MAKES: 1 cocktail

2   tablespoons chocolate syrup

3   ounces Baileys® Coffee liqueur

¾   cup milk

¾   cup seltzer

In a 12-ounce glass, stir together chocolate syrup, coffee liqueur, and milk. Top with seltzer and stir. Serve immediately.

LAVENDERTINI

SERVES: 15

COOK TIME: 5 minutes

- ½ cup sugar
- ½ tablespoon dried lavender
- 2¾ cups Smirnoff No. 21™ vodka
- ¼ cup crème de cassis
- 1 tablespoon curaçao
- 1 liter bottle sparkling water
  Lavender sprigs, for garnish

In a small pot over medium heat, dissolve sugar in ½ cup water. Bring to a boil, remove from the heat, and stir in the dried lavender. Let sit until cool and strain into a clean jar.

When ready to serve, in a pitcher stir together the vodka, cassis, and half the lavender sugar syrup. Stir a serving portion in a glass filled with ice until well chilled and strain into cold martini glasses, filling them about three-quarters full. Top with sparkling water and garnish with fresh lavender sprigs.

COCONUT RICE PUDDING

SERVES: 4

COOK TIME: 1 hour

- 3 cups cooked black rice
- ½ cup sugar
- 1 (13.5-ounce) can coconut milk, divided use
- 4 fortune cookies
- 1 cup white chocolate
- 2 tablespoons purple-colored sugar, for decoration

In a large pot, stir together the cooked rice with sugar and all but ¼ cup coconut milk. Bring to a simmer, reduce heat to low, and cook covered for 30 minutes, stirring occasionally, until rice is very soft and milk is thick.

While the rice pudding is cooking, melt the chocolate in the microwave, stopping to stir at 15-second intervals until melted. Place the colored sugar into a small bowl. Dip half of each fortune cookie in the white chocolate, then into the colored sugar, and place on wax paper–lined sheet tray. Allow chocolate to set in a cool place for about 30 minutes.

To serve, scoop rice pudding into serving glasses, drizzle with coconut milk, and serve with an embellished fortune cookie.

MANHATTAN MAN

MAKES: 1 cocktail

1   ounce Crown Royal® Deluxe whisky
½   ounce sweet vermouth
1   dash bitters
    Maraschino cherries, for garnish

To a cocktail shaker filled with ice, add whisky, sweet vermouth, and bitters. Shake and strain into a chilled martini glass. Garnish with maraschino cherries.

WHISKEY A GO GO

MAKES: 1 cocktail

1   ounce Bulleit® bourbon
½   ounce sweet vermouth
1   teaspoon maraschino cherry juice
    Sprig of mint
1   maraschino cherry, for garnish

Fill a cocktail shaker ¾ full with cracked ice. Add bourbon, sweet vermouth, and maraschino cherry juice. Shake with ice, strain into a chilled cocktail glass, and garnish with maraschino cherry and sprig of mint.

I LOVE YOU

MAKES: 1 cocktail

    Pink cocktail sugar
2   ounces cranberry juice
2   ounces champagne
    Maraschino cherry

Wet the rim of a champagne flute and dip it in pink sugar. Add cranberry juice and top with champagne. Garnish with a cherry.

SANDRA 75

MAKES: 4 cocktails

4   ounces Tanqueray® London Dry Gin
4   tablespoons cherry juice
8   dashes bitters
1   bottle chilled Stellina di Notte® Prosecco sparkling wine
4   frozen cherries, for garnish

Into each of four champagne flutes, add 1 ounce gin, 1 tablespoon cherry juice, and 2 dashes of bitters. Top each flute with sparkling wine and garnish with a cherry.

MARCH

Fruit Punch Fruit Tower
A Spring Affair Salsa
Sopes Strawberry Cream
Cookies Pretty Pink Cup
cake Soiree Fountain o
Cocktails Pretty Lemonade
Over the Rainbow Fruit
Punch Fruit Tower A Spring
Affair Salsa Sopes Straw
berry Cream Cookies
Pretty Pink Cupcake Soiree
Fountain of Cocktails
Pretty Lemonade Ove

Corset Cocktail: Shake 1 ounce Cîroc vodka, 1 dash Grand Marnier, 1½ ounces pink lemonade, and ½ ounce fresh lime juice over ice. Strain into a chilled champagne flute filled with ice. Top with champagne. Garnish with a rosebud.

FRUIT PUNCH

SERVES: 4

1   (15-ounce) can fruit cocktail in light
    syrup

½   cup Crown Royal® Deluxe whisky

1   (12-ounce) can pear nectar

1   (12-ounce) can peach nectar

Drain the fruit cocktail and reserve the syrup. Put the fruit into a bowl, pour in the whisky, and refrigerate for at least 1 hour.

In a pitcher, combine the reserved syrup with the nectars and refrigerate. Combine the fruit and whisky mixture with the nectar mixtures. Pour into ice-filled glasses and serve.

FRUIT TOWER

SERVES: 1

2   lemon slices
2   orange slices
2   clementine slices
2   lime slices
1   grapefruit slice

Stack fruit slices on top of each other to create a tower. Serve on a white plate.

SALSA SOPES

MAKES: 12 sopes

COOK TIME: 20 minutes

1 (18-ounce) package prepared polenta

2 tablespoons canola oil

1 (15-ounce) can black beans,
  rinsed & drained

1¼ cups jarred salsa

1 tablespoon, plus 2 teaspoons, hot sauce

½ cup sour cream

1 tablespoon lime juice

1 cup shredded lettuce

Slice the polenta in half. Slice each half into six rounds, about ½ inch thick, so you have 12 rounds total.

Heat oil in a large nonstick skillet over medium-high heat. Gently slide each polenta round into hot oil using a spatula. Fry for 5 minutes per side or until golden brown and cooked through. Remove from oil and drain on a paper towel–lined sheet tray.

In a medium bowl, combine beans, salsa, and 2 teaspoons hot sauce. Mash beans with a fork.

In a small bowl, combine the sour cream, remaining hot sauce, and lime juice and mix until well blended.

Spread 2 tablespoons mashed black beans on top of a fried polenta round. Top with a pinch of shredded lettuce and about 1 table-spoon of the salsa, and drizzle with some of the sour cream mixture.

A SPRING
AFFAIR

MAKES: 1 cocktail

1¼ ounces Smirnoff® Passion Fruit
Flavored vodka

¼ ounce almond liqueur

¾ ounce lime juice

¼ ounce Stirrings® grenadine

3 mint sprigs, for garnish

Build in a collins glass over ice. Garnish with
several mint sprigs.

STRAWBERRY CREAM COOKIES

MAKES: 24 cookies

COOK TIME: 8 minutes

1   (17.5-ounce) package sugar cookie mix

5   tablespoons butter, softened

1   egg white

5   tablespoons strawberry daiquiri mix,
    divided use

2   cups powdered sugar

Preheat oven to 375°F.

In a large mixing bowl, beat together the sugar cookie mix, butter, egg white, and 3 tablespoons strawberry daiquiri mix until dough is formed. Using a tablespoon measure, drop the dough out in cherry-size rounds onto a baking sheet. Bake until puffed, about 8 minutes. Allow to cool slightly on pan before transferring to a wire cooling rack to cool completely.

In a small bowl, combine the sugar with remaining daiquiri mix and whisk until blended. The filling should have a thick consistency. Spread a teaspoon of filling on the flat side of one of the cookies, and sandwich with a second. Repeat with remaining cookies and filling. Allow the filling to set.

PRETTY PINK

MAKES: 1 cocktail

- 1 ounce cherry brandy
- 1 ounce Smirnoff® Vanilla Flavored vodka
- 1 cup lemon-lime soda
  maraschino cherry, for garnish

In a collins glass filled with ice, combine vodka and cherry brandy. Top with lemon-lime soda. Garnish with a cherry.

CUPCAKE SOIREE

MAKES: 72 mini cupcakes
COOK TIME: 12 minutes

1	(18.25-ounce) box white cake mix, divided use
3	egg whites, divided use
9	tablespoons vegetable oil, divided use
⅓	cup plus 1 tablespoon blueberry juice, divided use
⅓	cup plus 1 tablespoon pineapple juice
⅓	cup plus 1 tablespoon cherry juice, divided use
2	sticks butter, softened
8	ounces cream cheese, softened
2	cups powdered sugar
	Red, blue, and yellow food coloring
24	fresh blueberries
12	pieces dried pineapple, sliced in half
12	maraschino cherries, stems removed

Preheat oven to 350°F and line 24-cup mini muffin tins with paper liners.

Evenly divide the cake mix into 3 bowls. In each bowl, add 1 egg white, 3 tablespoons oil, and ⅓ cup of one of the juices. Mix each for 2 minutes until batter is well incorporated. Scoop batter into muffin cups, filling each a little more than half full. Bake for 10 to 12 minutes. Remove from oven and place cupcakes on a wire rack to cool completely.

In a medium bowl, beat together the butter with cream cheese until combined. Slowly add in the powdered sugar until well incorporated. Evenly divide frosting between 3 bowls. Add 1 tablespoon of one of the juices to each and mix until well combined. Add 2 drops red food coloring to the cherry flavored, 2 drops of blue food coloring to the blueberry flavored, and 2 drops of yellow food coloring to the pineapple flavored. Mix until well combined.

Place each icing into a resealable plastic bag and snip off one of the bottom corners of each bag. Pipe each flavored frosting atop its corresponding cupcake. Garnish the top of each cupcake with its corresponding garnish.

FOUNTAIN OF COCKTAILS

SERVES: 10

1	quart blueberry juice
1	quart peach nectar
1	quart apple juice
1	quart cranberry juice
1	quart orange juice
1	quart pineapple juice
2	bottles Stellina di Notte® Prosecco sparkling wine, chilled

In a large pitcher, mix together the blueberry juice and peach nectar. In another large pitcher, mix together the apple and cranberry juices. In another large pitcher, mix together the orange and pineapple juices.

Fill glasses with your choice of juice and top with sparkling wine.

OVER THE RAINBOW

MAKES: 12 drinks

6   different flavors and colors of sports
    drinks, chilled
2   cups white grape juice, chilled
2   cups white cranberry juice, chilled
2   cups lemon-lime soda, chilled
12 ounces Smirnoff® Cranberry Flavored
    vodka, chilled

Pour sports drinks into ice cube trays
and freeze to make colored ice cubes. In a
2-quart pitcher, combine vodka, juices, and
soda. Fill glasses with rainbow ice cubes and
cover with punch.

PRETTY LEMONADE

SERVES: 8

1 pint fresh raspberries, plus more
for garnish

1 (12-ounce) can frozen concentrated
lemonade, thawed

1 lemon, sliced into thin rounds

1 quart Stirrings® club soda
Mint sprigs, for garnish

8 ounces Smirnoff® Raspberry
Flavored vodka

Using a rubber spatula, press the raspberries through a fine mesh sieve into a medium bowl. In a large pitcher, combine the frozen concentrated lemonade, strained raspberry puree, 1 quart of cold water, and the club soda. Stir and pour into glasses filled with ice. Garnish with a sprig of mint, a lemon slice, and fresh raspberries

APRIL

Stuffed Artichokes Ele
phant in the Room Frui
Bites Life Is Good Pea
Bella Delightfully Dicey
Ginger Sake Spritze
Cherry Clafoutis Daffodi
Parade Polka Dot Cocktai
Indochini Stuffed Arti
chokes Elephant in the
Room Fruit Bites Life Is
Good Pear Bella Delight
fully Dicey Ginger Sake
Spritzer Cherry Clafout

Sweet Lemon: Mix ¼ ounce triple sec, ¾ ounce lemon juice, and 1¼ ounces Smirnoff® No. 21 vodka. Shake with ice and strain into a pre-chilled goblet filled with crushed ice. Top with 1 ounce soda water. Garnish with a lemon twist. Makes 1 drink.

STUFFED ARTICHOKES

SERVES: 8

3　(14-ounce) cans whole artichoke
　　hearts
1　cup shredded red cabbage, grated
1　cup carrot, grated
2　scallions, finely sliced
¼　cup Italian dressing
　　Sesame seeds, for garnish
　　Kosher salt, to taste
　　Black pepper, to taste

Cut the top off each artichoke heart and pull out the center of each with your fingers to form a cup.

In a large bowl, toss together the cabbage, carrots, and scallions. Add the dressing and salt and pepper to taste. Fill the artichoke cups with the slaw, garnish with sesame seeds, and serve.

ELEPHANT IN THE ROOM

MAKES: 1 cocktail

- ¾ ounce white cranberry juice
- ¾ ounce Smirnoff® Strawberry Flavored vodka
- ½ ounce Smirnoff No. 21™ vodka
- ½ ounce Limoncello lemon liqueur

To a cocktail shaker full of ice, add all ingredients. Shake well and pour into chilled
martini glass.

FRUIT BITES

SERVES: 6

¼ cup honey mustard

2 teaspoons salt-free lemon and pepper seasoning

½ cup fat-free plain yogurt

1½ cups red seedless grapes

1 (6-ounce) package smoked ham slices, sliced in half and folded like an accordion

2 cups refrigerated precut mango chunks

2 cups refrigerated precut watermelon chunks

In a small bowl, combine mustard, lemon and pepper seasoning, and yogurt. Set aside, to be served with mango-melon bites.

Use a toothpick to skewer a grape, a folded half slice of ham, and a mango chunk or watermelon chunk. Repeat until all ingredients are used.

Serve with dipping sauce.

LIFE IS GOOD

MAKES: 6 cocktails

3   cups acai berry juice
2   cups Stirrings® Simple™ Margarita mix
1   cup Jose Cuervo Especial® tequila

In a pitcher, combine the acai berry juice, margarita mix, and tequila. Mix. Fill six margarita glasses with ice, pour in the margarita, and serve.

PEAR BELLA

MAKES: 2 cocktails

3 ounces Stirrings® Peach Bellini mix
1 ounce pear brandy
6½ ounces extra dry champagne

Stir together Bellini and pear brandy in a chilled glass. Divide into two rocks glasses filled with crushed ice. Top with chilled champagne.

DELIGHTFUL DICEY

MAKES: 1 cocktail

1½ ounces Crown Royal® Deluxe whisky
½ cup peach nectar, chilled
1 sprig fresh mint, for garnish

In a tall glass filled with ice, combine whisky and peach nectar. Stir and garnish with a mint sprig.

GINGER SAKE SPRITZER

SERVES: 4

1   (350 ml) bottle sake, chilled

1   liter bottle ginger ale, chilled

4   white sugar flowers, for garnish

In a pitcher, combine sake and ginger ale.
Pour into chilled martini glasses and
garnish with sugar flowers.

CHERRY CLAFOUTIS

SERVES: 8

COOK TIME: 1 hour

3 eggs

¾ cup sugar

¼ teaspoon salt

½ cup flour

2 tablespoons butter, melted and cooled

1 cup buttermilk

½ teaspoon almond extract

1 (12-ounce) package frozen pitted cherries, thawed and drained; set juice aside

¼ cup slivered almonds

1 cup French vanilla ice cream Confectioners' sugar, for garnish

Preheat oven to 350°F. Spray a deep 9-inch pie dish with nonstick cooking spray and place on a baking sheet.

In a large bowl, whisk together the eggs, sugar, salt, and flour until well combined. Whisk in the butter, buttermilk, and almond extract. Distribute cherries and ¼ cup almonds in bottom of pie dish in an even layer. Pour batter over cherries and bake for 45 minutes to 1 hour or until center is set and edges are golden.

Remove from oven and cool before slicing, about 30 minutes. To serve, in a microwave-safe bowl melt ice cream and warm slightly. Stir in reserved cherry juice. Spoon a few tablespoons onto a dessert plate, top with a slice of the clafoutis, and dust with confectioners' sugar.

DAFFODIL PARADE

MAKES: 1 cocktail

1½   ounces Smirnoff® Citrus Flavored
      vodka
3   ounces pineapple juice

In a cocktail shaker, combine vodka and
pineapple juice with plenty of ice. Cover
and shake vigorously. Strain into a chilled
martini glass.

POLKA DOT COCKTAIL

MAKES: 1 cocktail

1   ounce Cîroc® vodka
½   ounce blue curaçao
¼   ounce grapefruit juice
     Splash Stirrings® simple syrup

Fill a cocktail shaker with crushed ice. Add the vodka, curaçao, grapefruit juice, and simple syrup. Shake well, strain into a chilled martini glass, and serve.

INDOCHINI

MAKES: 2 cocktails

1   ounce blue tropical fruit liqueur
1½   ounces Smirnoff® Citrus Flavored
      vodka
1   tablespoon Stirrings® grenadine

Pour liqueur into the bottom of a chilled martini glass. To a cocktail shaker filled with ice, add vodka and shake. Gently pour chilled vodka into martini glass over the back of a spoon to avoid blending the liquors. Then gently pour the grenadine over the back of a spoon to create a layered effect. The grenadine will eventually bleed into the vodka and the blue liqueur.

MAY

Minty Mojito Capri Bites Rain Forest Nightcap Vineyard Spring Rolls Sake Shots Salty Dog Skinny Collins Roasted Shrimp Champagne Dreams R & R Tea Minty Mojito Capri Bites Rain Forest Nightcap Vineyard Spring Rolls Sake Shots Salty Dog Skinny Collins Roasted Shrimp

May Fiesta Rub rim of a chilled margarita glass with 1 lime wedge. Dip into 1 teaspoon salt to coat. To a shaker with ice, add 1 ounce Jose Cuervo® Especial Gold, 3 ounces Jose Cuervo® Lime Margarita Mix, a splash of pineapple juice, and a half handful of mint leaves. Shake vigorously and pour into margarita glass. Garnish with a lime peel. Makes 1 drink.

MINTY MOJITO

MAKES: 1 cocktail

1¼   ounces Myers's Platinum® rum
12   mint leaves, plus more for garnish
1   teaspoon sugar
½   ounce lime juice
2   ounces soda water

Place mint leaves in bottom of a tall glass. Add crushed ice, rum, sugar, and lime juice, and muddle. Add soda water and garnish with mint leaves.

CAPRI BITES

SERVES: 4

2   endives
1   large green or yellow tomato, chopped
1   cup grated mozzarella
¼   cup fresh basil, chopped
¼   cup balsamic vinaigrette salad dressing
¼   cup grated Parmesan cheese
    Kosher salt, to taste
    Black pepper, to taste

Separate the leaves of the endive and set aside the larger ones.

In a bowl, gently mix together the tomatoes, mozzarella, basil, and dressing, and season with salt and pepper to taste. Fill the prepared large endive leaves with the mixture. Sprinkle with a little Parmesan cheese.

RAIN FOREST NIGHTCAP

MAKES: 1 drink

1 ounce Johnnie Walker® Red Label®
   Scotch whisky

7 ounces brewed green tea

**In a mug, mix warm brewed tea with
Scotch. Serve with tea bag.**

VINEYARD

SERVES: 10

   1   large bunch green grapes
   2   liters lemon-lime soda, cold
 1½   cups Tanqueray® London Dry Gin
        Juice of 1 lemon
        Juice of 2 limes
        Lime wedges, for garnish

Pick the grapes from the stems and place
them in a single layer on a rimmed cookie
sheet. Put the grapes in the freezer for at
least 2 hours. Once frozen, the grapes can
be put into a plastic freezer bag.

When ready to serve, in a large pitcher stir
together the lemon-lime soda, gin, and lime
and lemon juices. Fill a glass with frozen
grapes and pour in the cocktail mix.
Garnish with slices of lime.

SPRING ROLLS

MAKES: 8 rolls
COOK TIME: 15 minutes

FOR THE SPRING ROLLS:

- 1 cup cooked shrimp, chopped
- 2 cups broccoli slaw
- 2 tablespoons sesame-ginger marinade
- 1 package spring roll wrappers
  Vegetable oil, for frying

FOR THE SPICY APRICOT MUSTARD DIP:

- 1 tablespoon sesame-ginger marinade
- ½ cup apricot preserves
- ¼ cup spicy brown mustard
- ½ teaspoon hot sauce

In a bowl, mix the shrimp, slaw, and marinade. Place a spring roll wrapper on your work surface with one of the corners facing you. Place 2 tablespoons of the filling on the third of the wrapper closest to you. Spread the filling out in a line from side to side, about an inch wide. Roll the corner of the wrapper nearest to you up over the filling, and then fold in the sides. Moisten the top corner with some water and roll the filling over it so it sticks to itself and forms a seal. Place seam-side down and keep covered with a damp towel while you make the remaining rolls.

Into a large heavy-bottomed pot pour enough oil to come up about 3 inches from the bottom. Place over medium-high heat and bring to 360°F. Add a few spring rolls and cook until they are golden brown, about 3 minutes. Drain on paper towels. Serve with the dipping sauce.

To make the Spicy Apricot Mustard Dip, in a small bowl, stir together the marinade, preserves, mustard, and hot sauce.

SAKE SHOTS

MAKES: 4 shots

1 large cucumber
1 ounce lime juice, freshly squeezed
1 tablespoon granulated sugar
4 ounces Myers's Platinum® white rum
1 ounce sake

To make cucumber shot glasses, cut four 2-inch-long pieces out of the cucumber. Use a melon baller to carefully scoop out flesh from one end, leaving a ½-inch bottom on the other end. Reserve cucumber flesh.

To make the sake shots, combine scooped-out cucumber flesh with lime juice in a blender. Blend until smooth, about 15 seconds. Pour cucumber puree through a fine-mesh strainer, reserving ½ cup of cucumber juice. Add sugar and set aside.

Pour raspberry rum and sake into a cocktail shaker filled with ice cubes. Add reserved cucumber juice and shake. Pour into cucumber shot glasses. Serve immediately.

SALTY DOG

MAKES: 1 cocktail

1   ounce Jose Cuervo Especial® tequila
3   ounces Jose Cuervo® Classic lime
     margarita mix
4   ounces crushed ice
1   teaspoon salt
     Lime wedges for garnish

Mix tequila, margarita mix, and ice in a
blender. Spread out salt on a plate. Rub the
rim of a chilled lowball glass with lime and
dip it into salt to frost. Pour mix into the
glass and garnish with a lime wedge.

SKINNY COLLINS

MAKES: 1 cocktail

1¼	ounces Tanqueray® London Dry Gin
1	ounce lemon juice
1	teaspoon sweet and sour mix
1	splash Stirrings® club soda
1	slice orange
1	maraschino cherry

In a cocktail shaker half filled with ice
cubes, add gin, lemon or lime juice, and
sweet and sour mix. Shake well. Strain into
a collins glass filled with ice. Add club soda
and stir well. Garnish with maraschino
cherry and orange slice.

ROASTED SHRIMP

SERVINGS: 4

COOK TIME: 6 minutes

1 pound (about 40) large shrimp, peeled, deveined, tails removed

1 cup roasted garlic salad dressing

1 teaspoon dried oregano

2 teaspoons lemon juice

1 (5-ounce) package baby arugula

2 plum tomatoes, diced

1 lemon, cut into wedges

Kosher salt, to taste

Black pepper, to taste

Soak eight 10-inch bamboo skewers in water for 30 minutes.

Thread shrimp onto the skewer through neck and tail portion. Use five shrimp per skewer. Place into a 9 × 13-inch baking dish and season with salt and pepper.

In a medium bowl, combine the roasted garlic salad dressing, oregano, and lemon juice. Reserve about 3 tablespoons of the salad dressing mixture. Pour the remaining dressing over the shrimp and, using a brush, make sure all the shrimp are completely coated with dressing. Let sit in refrigerator for 5 minutes.

Preheat a grill over medium-high heat.

Using a paper towel that has been soaked in canola oil, brush the grill grates with oil.

Place shrimp skewers on grill and cover. Cook until shrimp are cooked through, about 2 to 3 minutes per side.

While shrimp are grilling, combine the arugula and tomatoes in a large bowl. Pour the reserved dressing over the arugula and toss. Divide between four plates. Place two shrimp skewers on each plate. Serve with a lemon wedge on the side.

CHAMPAGNE DREAMS

MAKES: 2 cocktails

- 2 tablespoons cherry brandy
- 10 ounces extra dry champagne
- 2 maraschino cherries

Set out cocktail glasses. Add 1 tablespoon cherry brandy to each glass. Slowly pour in chilled champagne. Drop a cherry into each glass. Serve immediately.

R & R TEA

MAKES: 1 cocktail

1½ ounces Jeremiah Weed® Sweet-Tea
     Flavored vodka
2 cups frozen mixed berries

Simply pour the vodka over ice in a glass,
garnish with frozen berries, and serve in a
tall glass tea mug.

JUNE

Strawberry Licious Dai quiri Blushing Berry Cup cakes Caramel Banana Bliss Passion Fruit Punch Coconut Margarita Hawai ian Luau Pineapple Mai Tai Sparkling Orange Mo jito Margarita Lemon-Tini Glitterati Cakes Straw berry Licious Dai quiri Blushing Berry Cupcakes Caramel Banana Bliss Passion Fruit Punch

Phoenix Lemonade Fill glass with ice.
Add 1½ ounces Smirnoff® Twist of Citrus
vodka and 4 ounces lemonade. Stir
well. Garnish with an orange twist.
Makes 1 drink.

STRAWBERRY LICIOUS DAIQUIRI

MAKES: 1 cocktail

1½ ounces Jose Cuervo Especial® tequila

3 ounces Jose Cuervo® Classic Lime margarita mix

1 handful fresh strawberries

4 ounces crushed ice

1 teaspoon sugar

In a blender, combine tequila, margarita mix, strawberries, and ice. Mix until smooth. Pour into a margarita glass and garnish with a strawberry.

BLUSHING BERRY CUPCAKES

MAKES: 48 mini cupcakes
COOK TIME: 15 minutes

FOR CUPCAKES:

- 1 pound strawberries, washed and hulled
- 1 (18.25-ounce) box white cake mix
- 3 egg whites
- ⅓ cup canola oil

FOR FROSTING:

- 2 egg whites
- 1 cup sugar
- ¼ cup strawberry puree, reserved
- 1 tablespoon light corn syrup
- 1 teaspoon vanilla extract
- Red food coloring

TO MAKE CUPCAKES:

Preheat oven to 350°F. Line two 24-count mini-muffin tins.

In a blender, combine the strawberries (reserve about 12 small strawberries for garnish, slicing each into 4) with ¼ cup water and puree until smooth. Set aside ¼ cup puree for frosting.

In a large mixing bowl, beat together the cake mix, egg whites, canola oil, and 1½ cups pureed strawberries for 2 minutes, until well incorporated. Fill muffin tins about three-quarters of the way. Bake for 8 minutes or until tops are golden. Remove from oven. Cool slightly before removing from pan and cooling completely.

TO MAKE FROSTING:

In a mixing bowl that fits over top of a pot of boiling water, combine all ingredients except the vanilla and food coloring. Beat with handheld mixer on medium speed while mixture cooks for about 7 minutes until peaks are formed. Remove from heat, add vanilla, and color with red food coloring to desired shade of pink. Frost cupcakes with the colored frosting and garnish each cupcake with a strawberry slice.

CARAMEL BANANA BLISS

MAKES: 8 taquitos

COOK TIME: 10 minutes

8   small flour tortillas

1   large banana

½   (13.4-ounce) can dulce de leche

½   cup shredded coconut

1   cup chocolate fudge topping

¼   cup brewed decaffeinated coffee

    Canola oil for frying

Wrap the tortillas in a damp paper towel and microwave on high for 45 seconds. Cut banana in half crosswise. Slice each half lengthwise into quarters, forming sticks 3 inches long. Lay a tortilla on a flat surface. Spread a thin layer of dulce de leche over tortilla, stopping ½ inch from edge. Sprinkle with 1 tablespoon coconut. Place a slice of banana near edge, roll up tortilla, and secure closed with a tooth-pick. Repeat with remaining tortillas.

In a large skillet, heat enough oil to come ½ inch up the side of the pan over medium-high heat. When oil is at 350°F, place tortilla rolls seam-side down in the oil and fry in batches for 1 minute per side until golden brown. Remove from oil and drain on a paper towel–lined plate or sheet pan.

Stir hot coffee together with fudge topping. Remove toothpicks from tortillas, and drizzle with some of the chocolate sauce.

PASSION FRUIT PUNCH

SERVES: 6

½   cup passion fruit syrup, Torani®

½   cup peach nectar

1   liter orange-flavored seltzer

1   cup Myers's Platinum® White rum
    (optional)
    Ice cubes

In a large pitcher, combine syrup, nectar, and seltzer. Add rum (optional) and ice cubes. Stir well. Pour into highball glasses.

COCONUT MARGARITA

SERVES: 5

COOK TIME: 5 minutes

½ cup sugar

2½ cups coconut water, divided use

½ cup Captain Morgan Parrot Bay®
Coconut rum

¼ cup Jose Cuervo Especial® tequila

¼ cup Godiva® White Chocolate liqueur

2 tablespoons lime juice

¼ cup sweetened flaked coconut

In a small pot over medium heat, combine ½ cup coconut water with sugar. Heat until sugar has dissolved to make simple syrup. Remove from heat and allow to cool.

Dip rims of 4 lowball glasses into coconut syrup. Place coconut shavings in a small plate and invert glasses into coconut to coat the rims, then fill the glasses with ice.

In a pitcher, combine remaining coconut water, rum, tequila, and white chocolate liqueur with 2 tablespoons of coconut simple syrup and lime juice. Stir and pour into rimmed glasses.

HAWAIIAN LUAU

MAKES: 2 drinks

- 2 ounces melon liqueur
- 1 ounce Captain Morgan Parrot Bay®
  Coconut rum
- 1 ounce Stirrings® triple sec
- 1 cup pineapple juice
  Fresh pineapple wedges
  Pineapple leaves
  Orange slices, quartered

Fill two tall glasses with ice. Pour 1 ounce melon liqueur over ice in each glass. Add ½ ounce coconut rum and ½ ounce triple sec to each glass. Fill glasses with pineapple juice. Garnish with pineapple wedges, pineapple leaves, and orange slices.

PINEAPPLE MAI TAI

MAKES: 1 cocktail

- 1 ounce Bulleit® bourbon
- 2 ounces orange juice
- 1 ounce pineapple juice
- ¼ ounce Stirrings® grenadine
- 1 slice pineapple

Fill a cocktail shaker with ice. Add orange juice, pineapple juice, grenadine, and bourbon. Shake and strain into an ice-filled highball glass. Garnish with a pineapple slice and cocktail umbrella.

SPARKLING ORANGE

SERVES: 11

1	bottle Stellina Di Notte® Prosecco
1¼	cups Captain Morgan® Original Spiced rum
3	cups orange juice
4	dashes Stirrings® Blood Orange bitters
	Sliced orange, for garnish

In a pitcher, combine rum, orange juice, and bitters. Pour into champagne flutes, filling each about halfway. Top with sparkling wine and garnish with an orange slice.

MOJITO MARGARITA

MAKES: 2 cocktails

	Granulated sugar
½	lime, cut into quarters
3	ounces Jose Cuervo Especial® tequila
⅔	cup Stirrings® Simple™ Mojito
3	tablespoons bottled lime juice
1	cup medium ice cubes
6	fresh raspberries

Spread a thin layer of sugar on a saucer. Run a lime wedge around rim of each of 2 chilled margarita or martini glasses. Press rims into sugar to create narrow sugared edge on each glass.

In a cocktail shaker, combine tequila, mojito mixer, lime juice, and ice cubes. Shake vigorously. Strain equal amounts into each margarita glass. Squeeze juice from 1 lime wedge into each drink. Garnish with 3 fresh raspberries each.

LEMON-TINI

SERVES: 4

3   ounces Limoncello lemon liqueur
4½ ounces Smirnoff® Citrus
    Flavored vodka
½   cup lemonade
    Sparkling water, chilled
    Lemon slices, for garnish

In a pitcher filled with ice, pour in the Limon-cello, vodka, and lemonade and stir. Strain the drink evenly into the four prepared glasses. Top with sparkling water and lemon slice and serve.

GLITTERATI CAKES

MAKES: 24 cupcakes
COOK TIME: 12 minutes

1   (18.25-ounce) box white cake mix
1⅓ cups buttermilk
3   egg whites
2   (16-ounce) cans white frosting
     Pearl dragées
     Pearl luster dust
1   (16-ounce) package ready-to-use
     gum paste
     1-inch vine leaf-shaped
     gum-paste cutter

Preheat oven to 350°F. Line two 12-cup muffin tins with paper liners.

Make cake mix according to package instructions, substituting buttermilk for water in recipe. Fill each cupcake liner ⅔ the way to the top. Bake in oven, rotating pans halfway, for 10 to 12 minutes. Tops will be golden and toothpick inserted in center will come out clean when done. Remove from oven and cool slightly before removing from pan to cool completely.

For the leaves, knead and roll out the gum paste to ¹⁄₁₆-inch thickness. Using the leaf cutter, cut 24 leaves. Using the back end of a butter knife, make leaf veins by pressing lightly into paste. Set out on a tray lined with a wrinkled piece of plastic wrap to dry.

To decorate, ice each cupcake using an off-set spatula with a swirled top. Sprinkle with pearl dragées. Using a clean paintbrush, dust leaf with luster dust and place one atop each cupcake.

JULY

Campsite Shortcake
Stars and Stripes Jalapeño
Poppers All-American
Cranberry Margarita A Red
Berry Blueberry Mojito
Old Blue Eyes Vanilla-Ras
Napoleon Cool Coconut
Bubble Tea Star-Tin
Campsite Shortcake Stars
and Stripes Jalapeño
Poppers All-American
Cranberry Margarita A Red

Summer Jubilee: Mix ¾ ounce Sterling Vineyards® chardonnay, ¾ ounce Cîroc® vodka, and ¼ ounce peach schnapps. Shake with ice and strain into a prechilled wineglass. Stir in ¼ cup diced strawberries and ⅛ cup blueberries. Top with 1 ounce lemon-lime soda. Garnish with a strawberry. Makes 1 drink.

CAMPSITE SHORTCAKE

SERVES: 4

COOK TIME: 10 minutes

2	ciabatta sandwich loaves
4	tablespoons unsalted butter, melted
¼	cup sugar
2	teaspoons ground pumpkin pie spice
1	pint strawberries, sliced
½	pint blueberries
½	pint raspberries
	Juice and zest of a lemon
1	(8-ounce) tub whipped topping
	Mint, for garnish

Preheat grill to medium heat.

In a small bowl, combine the sugar and pumpkin pie spice.

Slice each loaf lengthwise. Brush cut sides of bread with melted butter and sprinkle with half of the sugar mixture. Place on grill and grill until toasted.

In another large bowl, combine berries with half the lemon juice and remaining 2 tablespoons sugar-and-spice mixture. Allow berries to sit and macerate for 15 minutes.

Combine the remaining lemon juice and zest with the whipped topping and stir.

Remove bread from grill. Top each half with ½ cup of the berry mixture. Serve with a dollop of lemon whipped topping and garnish with mint.

STARS AND STRIPES

SERVES: 6

2	hibiscus tea bags	Brew tea with 3 cups of hot water. Cool to room temperature and chill in refrigerator, about 30 minutes.
2	cups lemonade	
¾	cup gin	
¼	cup orange liqueur	
¼	cup Stirrings® grenadine	In a large pitcher, combine tea, lemonade, gin, and orange liqueur and stir well to combine. Pour into glass mugs filled with ice. Top each with a tablespoon of grenadine.

JALAPEÑO POPPERS

MAKES: 12 poppers
COOK TIME: 15 minutes

12   jalapeño peppers
 3   cheddar cheese sticks
 6   pieces bacon, cut in half
 1   tablespoon chili powder
 2   tablespoons cream cheese, softened
 ¼   cup sour cream
 2   tablespoons honey

Soak 12 wooden toothpicks in water for 30 minutes.

Preheat a grill to medium heat.

Cut off stem end of jalapeño peppers. Scrape out the seeds and ribs from the inside.

Slice each cheese stick in half crosswise and then cut each half in half lengthwise. Stuff each pepper with a piece of cheese. Wrap each stuffed pepper with a piece of bacon and secure with a toothpick. Sprinkle with chili powder.

Place on grill, cover, and cook over indirect heat for 13 minutes, until bacon is crispy, turning every 3 minutes.

While poppers are grilling, combine the cream cheese, sour cream, and honey in a small bowl. Mix well and serve with the poppers.

ALL-AMERICAN

MAKES: 1 cocktail

1½   ounces Smirnoff® Green Apple
       Flavored vodka
3   ounces cranberry juice

**Fill tall glass with ice cubes. Add vodka
and cranberry juice. Stir well.**

CRANBERRY MARGARITA

MAKES: 1 cocktail

1 ounce Jose Cuervo Especial® tequila

1 ounce cranberry juice

¼ cup whole berry cranberry sauce

½ ounce orange liqueur

10 ice cubes

Dried cranberries, for garnish

Lime slice, for garnish

Combine all ingredients, except dried cranberries and lime wedge, in blender. Blend on high setting until smooth. Serve in a margarita glass. Garnish with dried cranberries and a lime slice.

A RED BERRY

MAKES: 1 cocktail

1½   ounces Jose Cuervo Especial® tequila

3   ounces Jose Cuervo® Classic Lime
     margarita mix

1   handful fresh strawberries

4   ounces crushed ice

     Sprig of fresh mint, for garnish

In a blender, combine tequila, margarita mix, strawberries, and ice. Mix until smooth. Pour into a stemmed glass and garnish with a mint sprig.

OLD BLUE EYES

MAKES: 1 cocktail

1½   ounces blue curaçao
     Splash of lemonade
3   blueberries

Mix blue curaçao in the glass with a splash of lemonade and drop three blueberries in the glass to garnish.

BLUEBERRY MOJITO

SERVES: 8

1 cup blueberries, plus more for garnish

1 bottle ready-to-serve Smirnoff® vodka mojito

1 liter Stirrings® soda water

8 sprigs fresh mint, for garnish.

In a large pitcher, add the blueberries and muddle until they release their juices. Pour in the ready-to-serve mojito vodka and soda water and stir. Pour into tall glasses filled with ice. Garnish with a mint sprig and a few blueberries and serve.

VANILLA-RAS NAPOLEON

SERVES: 4

2   tablespoons honey

2   tablespoons raspberry fruit spread

1   teaspoon vanilla extract, divided use

1   pint fresh raspberries, reserve 4
    raspberries for garnish

3   (3.75-ounce) vanilla pudding cups

2   (3.5-ounce) boxes butter crisp
    wafer cookies

In a small bowl, gently stir together the honey, fruit spread, and ½ teaspoon vanilla. Add raspberries and toss to coat.

In a medium bowl, mix together the pudding and remaining vanilla extract.

To assemble, place a wafer cookie onto a plate. Top with 1 heaping tablespoon of the pudding and 1 heaping tablespoon of the raspberries and a second wafer cookie. Top with another heaping tablespoon of the pudding and another heaping tablespoon of the raspberries and then a third wafer cookie. Top with a dollop of the pudding and garnish with a reserved raspberry. Repeat with remaining ingredients.

COOL COCONUT

SERVES: 4

¾ cup cream of coconut

2 cups pear juice

¼ cup lime juice

1 (12-ounce) can seltzer

6 ounces Myers's Platinum® white rum

In a small pitcher, combine the cream of
coconut, pear juice, lime juice, and seltzer
and stir well. Pour into tall glasses filled with
crushed ice. Add ¼ cup of rum per drink if
desired. Serve with a straw.

BUBBLE TEA

SERVES: 4

COOK TIME: 25 minutes

1   cup sugar
1   cup large tapioca pearls
6   jasmine tea bags
½   cup sweetened condensed milk
4   ounces Smirnoff No. 21™ vodka

Combine sugar and 1 cup of water in a small pot. Bring to a boil over medium heat to make simple syrup. Remove from heat and set aside to cool.

In a large pot over high heat, boil 8 cups of water. Add the tapioca pearls, return to the boil, and cook, stirring occasionally, for 15 minutes. Turn off the heat, cover, and let the pearls sit for another 15 minutes. Drain and rinse under cold water. Put into a container with the simple syrup.

Put the tea bags into a heatproof container and pour 4 cups of boiling water over them. Let steep for 20 minutes, remove the bags, and discard them. Let the tea cool, then refrigerate.

When you are ready to serve, put ¼ cup of tapioca pearls into the bottom of a large glass. In a pitcher, combine vodka, tea, and sweetened condensed milk and stir until blended. Pour over the pearls and serve.

STAR-TINI

MAKES: 4 cocktails

4   ounces Smirnoff No. 21™ vodka
    Ice
2   ounces orange liqueur
2   ounces white cranberry juice
2   lime wedges
    Orange slices and star fruit slices

Fill a cocktail shaker with ice. Pour vodka, orange liqueur, and cranberry juice over ice;
squeeze in juice from lime wedges. Cover and
shake. Strain into 4 chilled martini glasses.
Garnish with orange and star fruit slices.

AUGUST

Shoreline Sliders Sassy
Sangria Lush Lemon
Mango Sorbet Porch
Swing Iced Tea Orange
Cherry Strawberry Nirvana
Marshmallow Shooters
Maypole Punch Cherry
Pink Lady Mint Chip
Grasshopper Golden
Cream Cadillac Blue
Cheese Pear Bites Root-
Beer Floats Shoreline
Sliders Sassy Sangria

Mystic Mojito: In a cocktail shaker, combine 3 ounces Stirrings® Mojito Mixer, 1½ ounces Myers's Platinum® White rum, and 1 cup ice. Cover and shake vigorously. Add 3 ounces club soda and mix gently. Pour into a cocktail glass and garnish with a wedge of lime and a sprig of mint. Makes 1 drink.

SHORELINE SLIDERS

MAKES: 8 sliders
COOK TIME: 6 minutes

1½ pounds salmon fillet, skin removed
1 tablespoon lemon-and-pepper seasoning
¼ cup canola oil
2 tablespoons red wine vinegar
2 tablespoons spicy brown mustard
1 teaspoon sugar
1 (6-ounce) bag shredded red cabbage
2 scallions, sliced
¼ cup tartar sauce
¼ cup sweet chili sauce
¼ cup whipped cream cheese, softened
8 mini buns
   Kosher salt, to taste
   Black pepper, to taste

Preheat grill to medium-high heat.

Cut salmon fillet into 2-inch squares so that you get 8 portions. Season both sides of each salmon fillet with lemon and pepper seasoning.

Brush the grill grate with a paper towel that has been soaked in canola oil. Grill salmon 3 minutes per side or until just cooked through.

In a large bowl, whisk together the vinegar, mustard, and sugar. Add cabbage and sliced scallions and toss to coat.

In a small bowl, stir together the tartar sauce, sweet chili sauce, and cream cheese.

Spread about 1 teaspoon of sauce on the tops of the buns. Place salmon on bun and top with crispy slaw.

SASSY SANGRIA

SERVES: 12

3	cups red wine, BV Coastal Estates® Cabernet
1	cup brandy
¼	cup Stirrings® triple sec
1	orange, sliced
1	lime, sliced
1	lemon, sliced
1	apple, cored and diced
8	fresh raspberries
2	cups Stirrings® club soda

In a large pitcher, combine all ingredients
except club soda. Cover tightly and
refrigerate 3 hours.

Pour ¾ cup sangria mixture and ¼ cup club
soda into each squall glass, dividing fruit
equally. Serve immediately.

LUSH LEMON

SERVES: 4

4 lemons
½ pint lemon sorbet
4 ounces Limoncello, chilled
3½ ounces Smirnoff® Vanilla Flavored
    vodka, chilled

Cut the top third off each lemon and reserve. Cut a small slice off the bottom of each lemon so it stands up. Using a spoon, carefully scoop out the inside of each lemon, leaving a lemon cup to serve in. Put the cups and tops in the freezer for 1 hour.

Put the sorbet into the bowl of a food processor. Add the Limoncello and vodka and process until smooth. Fill the lemon shells with the mixture and put them back into the freezer to firm up for 1 to 2 hours. Put the tops on and serve.

MANGO SORBET

MAKES: 1 quart sorbet

1 pound frozen mango chunks, chopped
1 red jalapeño, stemmed, seeded, and finely chopped
1 green jalapeño, stemmed, seeded, and finely chopped
2 (11.5-ounce) cans mango nectar

In a large bowl, combine all ingredients and let sit for 30 minutes.

Pour mixture into a 1-quart ice cream maker and freeze according to manufacturer's instructions.

Serve immediately.

PORCH SWING ICED TEA

MAKES: 1 drink

Ice cubes

1½ ounces Smirnoff® Citrus Flavored vodka

1 cup iced tea

Mint sprigs

Fill a highball glass with ice cubes. Pour in vodka and your favorite iced tea. Garnish with sprigs of mint and serve.

ORANGE CHERRY

MAKES: 5 cocktails

6 ounces Myers's Platinum® White Rum

1½ ounces Grand Marnier orange liqueur

6 ounces orange juice

6 ounces pineapple juice

1½ ounces lime juice

1½ ounces Stirrings® simple syrup

4 dashes bitters

2 ounces Stirrings® grenadine

3 maraschino cherries per cocktail

To a cocktail shaker with ice, add the rum, Grand Marnier, orange juice, pineapple juice, lime juice, simple syrup, bitters, and grenadine. Shake and strain into ice-filled highball glasses. String a toothpick with maraschino cherries and place across the top of each glass for garnish.

STRAWBERRY NIRVANA

MAKES: 1 cocktail

- 4 ounces ice
- 1½ ounces Smirnoff® Strawberry Flavored vodka
- 1 handful strawberries
- 2 slices banana, for garnish

Add ice, vodka, and strawberries to a blender and blend well. Pour into a tall glass, and garnish with a strawberry and banana slices.

MARSHMALLOW
SHOOTERS

SERVES: 4

1 pint vanilla ice cream

1 cup milk

½ cup marshmallow cream

½ cup Godiva® White Chocolate liqueur

In a blender, add the ice cream, milk, marshmallow cream, and chocolate liqueur, and blend until smooth. Serve in shooter glasses.

MAYPOLE PUNCH

MAKES: 24 servings

1 cup frozen peach slices, Dole®
1 cup frozen whole strawberries
¼ cup fresh mint leaves
1 (46-ounce) can pineapple juice, divided
½ cup frozen orange juice concentrate
2 cups frozen sliced strawberries, thawed
2 (11.5 ounce) cans peach nectar
4 cups lemon-lime soda
1 bottle chilled Stellina di Notte® Prosecco sparkling wine (optional)

Arrange a double layer of peaches, strawberries, and mint leaves in the bottom of a Bundt pan. Add enough pineapple juice to cover fruit. Freeze for at least 2 hours or until set.

In a large punch bowl, combine remaining ingredients, except sparkling wine. Stir to mix thoroughly.

To serve, remove Bundt pan from freezer. Unmold ice ring and float in center of punch bowl. Ladle punch into glasses. Top punch with champagne.

ICE CREAM COCKTAILS

EACH RECIPE MAKES: 1 cocktail

CHERRY PINK LADY

- 1 ounce Smirnoff® Vanilla Flavored vodka
- ½ ounce black raspberry liqueur
- ½ ounce Stirrings® grenadine
- 2 scoops vanilla ice cream
  Pressurized whipped cream
- 1 maraschino cherry

Place vodka, raspberry liqueur, grenadine, and ice cream in a blender. Blend until thick and creamy. Pour into a glass. Garnish with whipped cream and a cherry.

GOLDEN CREAM CADILLAC

- ½ ounce Galliano® liqueur
- ½ ounce Stirrings® triple sec
- 1 ounce white crème de cacao
  Splash orange juice, Minute Maid®
- 2 scoops vanilla ice cream
  Pressurized whipped cream

Place all ingredients except whipped cream in a blender. Blend until thick and creamy. Pour into a glass and top with whipped cream.

MINT CHIP GRASSHOPPER

- 1 ounce green crème de menthe
- 1 ounce white crème de cacao
- 2 scoops vanilla ice cream
  Pressurized whipped cream
  Fresh mint sprig

Place crème de menthe, crème de cacao, and ice cream into a blender. Blend until thick and creamy. Pour into a glass. Garnish with whipped cream and a sprig of mint.

BLUE CHEESE PEAR BITES

SERVES: 4

COOK TIME: 8 minutes

2 tablespoons unsalted butter

1 pear, thinly sliced

½ cup frozen chopped onions

2 teaspoons lemon juice

4 slices pumpernickel bread, toasted and each slice cut into quarters

1 cup crumbled blue cheese

¼ cup white chocolate shavings

Kosher salt, to taste

Black pepper, to taste

Preheat the broiler on low.

In a large skillet over medium-high heat, add butter. When the butter has melted add the pear slices, onions, lemon juice, and a pinch each of salt and pepper. Cook until the pears are warmed through and soft but still hold together, about 5 minutes.

Place the toast squares onto a baking sheet. Lay a few slices of pear in a single layer on each toast square. Top with the crumbled blue cheese. Place under the broiler until the cheese begins to melt, about 1 minute. Transfer to a platter, garnish with a sprinkle of the white chocolate shavings, and serve immediately.

ROOT-BEER FLOATS

MAKES: 1 float

1	scoop vanilla ice cream
1½	ounces Smirnoff® Vanilla Vodka
1	liter bottle root beer
2	ounces chocolate syrup

Scoop vanilla ice cream into a tall glass. Pour vodka or chocolate syrup over ice cream. Fill tall glass mug with root beer.

Credits

PHOTOGRAPHY:

Cocktail and food photographs by
Ed Ouellette

Photographs by Ben Fink on pp. i, ii, iv, v, x,
xi, xii, xiii, xiv, xv, xvi, xvii, 3, 19, 33, 51, 69, 83,
97, 109, 121, 135, 149, 153, and 179

PHOTO RETOUCHING:

Gary Noel

PROP STYLING:

Penelope Bouklas and Rich Vassilatos

FOOD STYLING:

Jamie Kimm and Christina Pichler

HAIR:

Laurent Saint Cricq

MAKEUP:

Frank Guytom

WARDROBE STYLING:

Amit Gajwani and Annie Semenczuk

WARDROBE DESIGNERS:

Badgley Mischka

Ted Baker London

Carmen Marc Valvo

Max Studio

Moritz Glik

Judith Ripka

Jussara Lee

Jay Godfrey

Isaac Mizrahi

Soigne K

Katie Decker

Vibes

Index

Add Your Own Recipes Here

Add Your Own Recipes Here

Add Your Own Recipes Here

....

....

....

....

....

....

....

....

....

....

....

Add Your Own Recipes Here